new country garden

new country garden

ELSPETH THOMPSON
MELANIE ECLARE

RYLAND
PETERS
& SMALL

LONDON NEW YORK

First published in the United Kingdom in 2001
by Ryland Peters & Small
20–21 Jockey's Fields
London WC1R 4BW
www.rylandpeters.com

This compact edition published 2005

10 9 8 7 6 5 4 3 2 1

Text © 2001, 2005 Elspeth Thompson.
Design and photographs © 2001, 2005 Ryland
Peters & Small. The following photographs ©
Melanie Eclare: 63l, 64–65, 72r–73l, 78l, 99r, 118l,
119r, 121ar, 122l, 122r–123 all, 126b, 127l, 128r,
129, 130, 131l, 131r, 132, 133al, 134-135, 137r.

For this edition
Senior designer Steve Painter
Senior editor Clare Double
Picture research Tracy Ogino
Production Gavin Bradshaw
Art director Gabriella Le Grazie
Publishing director Alison Starling
UK Locations Melanie Eclare and
            Elspeth Thompson

For Frank and Tom

Text by Elspeth Thompson
All photographs by Melanie Eclare

Front cover photograph: Niall Manning and Alastair
Morton's garden, Dunard, Fintry, Scotland. Back
jacket: left Peter and Sandra Aitken-Quack's
garden at Ham Cross Farm near Tisbury, designed
by Tania Compton; right Marc Schoellen's garden in
Luxembourg, called 'La Bergerie'.

ISBN 1 84172 878 0

A CIP record for this book is available from the
British Library.

Printed and bound in China

contents

introduction

Until recently, the words 'new' and 'country' were not often heard together. For too long, we have tended to associate the country with all things traditional, and have looked for innovation in cities and towns. In gardening terms, 'country' has meant either old-fashioned cottage gardens, with familiar flowers and vegetables grown together in a colourful jumble, or a much grander style, where formal designs or naturalistic parkland linked large country houses with the landscape beyond.

Much has been made of today's renaissance in gardening: the flurry of new interest, in particular among young people, and the creation of stunning new gardens with a distinctive modern style. There is no doubt that garden design has caught up with architecture, interior design and fashion to become a truly contemporary form of expression. But most of the celebrated new gardens are town gardens – tiny spaces transformed into trendy outdoor dining rooms, or urban jungles crammed full of exotic plants and city salvage. You'd be forgiven for thinking that new ideas stopped short at the city limits. Meanwhile, however, another strand of garden design has been quietly taking root. Country dwellers have been just as inspired by recent developments in gardening, and have been creating wonderful gardens that are as exciting – and influential – as their urban counterparts. Call it new country, call it modern rustic, call it what you will – this new style of gardening has more to do with attitude and aesthetics than geographical location. And it is here to stay.

The new country garden hasn't turned its back on tradition entirely. You won't find here the plastic gardens, glass gardens, or metal and microchip gardens hailed as horticultural flavour of the month on television and in magazines. New materials undoubtedly have a place in the new country garden – concrete, slate and shiny new metal among them – but these are peaceful, laid-back places, where the important things in life such as beauty, comfort and romance are not forgotten. The emphasis is on enjoyment: of the beautiful views beyond the boundary; of the changing atmospheres created by contrasting features and spaces; of the colours, shapes and textures of the plants themselves. Unlike many of the new urban gardens, these are gardeners' gardens. Their owners may not all be experts – although many of them are – but they are all united by a real love of plants and the magic they can weave. Yards of decking and limestone remain static and soulless without the textures, scents and shadows of well-chosen plants. And low-maintenance gardening is all very well – but where are the flowers?

Plants remain the real heart of the country-style garden. But you can forget about pastel sweet peas and pink cabbage roses. The palette and range of plants has been revolutionized, with bold clashing colours and a striking mix of heights and textures that breaks all the old rules. You'll find wildflower meadows, banks of ornamental grasses swaying in the breeze, even geometric beds filled with black and white irises – but what you won't find are plants that will struggle in the prevailing conditions. New country gardeners work with nature, not against it. And happy plants make a happy garden.

Design naturally plays a part in the new country garden – but never in an imposing, insensitive way that forgets the real purpose of the place. Gardens are to be looked at, certainly, but they are also to be lived in and enjoyed – not only by their creators and their families, friends and pets, but also by birds and other wildlife. The new country style fuses contemporary ideas with honest local materials to create spaces and features that relate to a relaxed and flexible modern way of life. It doesn't matter where you live – if you have ever longed for a pond buzzing with dragonflies, a swing in a tree overgrown with clematis and roses, or a modernday potager full of fresh organic vegetables, the new country garden is for you.

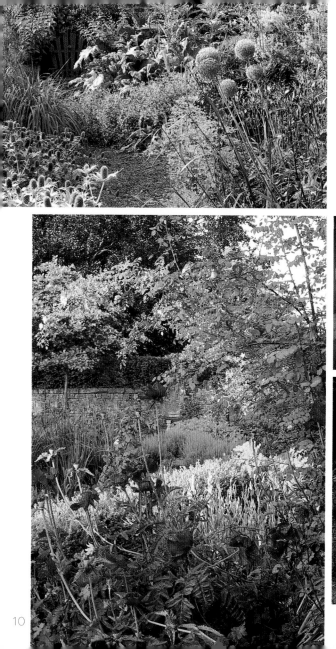

Left This cutting garden contains an exciting mix of large-scale plants, among them the silver Miss Willmott's ghost (*Eryngium giganteum*) and the huge purple spheres of *Allium giganteum* (foreground).

Below left The splendid deep red blooms of the tall poppy *Papaver orientale* Goliath Group stand out against a green backdrop in this courtyard garden.

Below *Rosa* 'Lilli Marlene'.

a plant lover's paradise

Plants remain the heroes of the country-style garden: the heart and soul of the place and the real passion of its creators. But the palette of plants grown in these gardens has undergone a transformation. Colours are stronger and textures are bolder, while ornamental grasses bring a new sense of movement to beds and borders.

Traditional cottage garden plants – sweet peas, hollyhocks, delphiniums and love-in-a-mist – are familiar to us all from old photographs and watercolours. Arranged with the tallest plants against the house wall and the rest in clouds of pastel pinks and blues in front, they create a picturesque patchwork that peaks in midsummer. The other timeless country garden image is the classic herbaceous border – strictly ordered in terms of height and subtle shifts of colour, and requiring a lot of maintenance. The new country garden takes the best from each of these traditional planting styles, but adds something of its own. Planting is bigger and bolder and breaks many of the old rules.

First, though, one of the most important lessons to re-learn from the old cottage gardeners is only to grow plants that will thrive

Left A modern colour mix in this impressive long border in Ireland, with its confident combination of bright shades and contrasting textures. The shaggy yellow daisies of *Inula hookeri* take up the rear, soaking up the sun behind mauve Michaelmas daisies, flaming orange crocosmias, delicate white spires of *Veronicastrum virginicum* and pink *Sidalcea malviflora*. The white flowers take on a luminous quality in the full sun, and the crocosmias' spear-like leaves are shot the brightest lime green.

Above Bold planting in terms of height, shape and colour prevails in this garden in East Sussex, specially created to provide flowers for cutting and arranging. Towering onopordums and cardoons are silhouetted against the sky, their scrolling silvery foliage providing a foil for the brilliant colours of the flowers – bright orange lilies, lime-green euphorbias and violet alliums.

in your conditions. The new country gardener is not interested in trying to grow rhododendrons or heather on chalky soil – in fact, he or she is probably not interested in growing rhododendrons or heather at all. Gardeners are resourceful souls – and over the years have found ways to create artificial conditions in even the most unpromising soils and sites – but in recent years there has been a welcome return to the principles of suiting your planting to your surroundings. Natural-looking plants that at least give the impression they might be indigenous to the area now hold sway. Inspired by examples such as Beth Chatto's gravel and damp gardens in East Anglia and the designer Isabelle Greene's work in arid California, gardeners are realizing that there is no substitute for a plant that is truly happy in its natural habitat. Growth will be stronger, flowers

Above Soft plumes of the Mexican feather grass *Stipa tenuissima* catch the light amid clouds of pale pink astrantia. The delicate starry flowers and wispy grass complement each other perfectly in this stunning wild garden in Dorset.
Left Bright red *Persicaria amplexicaulis*, fuzzy mauve Joe Pye weed (*Eupatorium purpureum*) and purple monardas form bold swathes towards the back of this border, a splendid contrast with the lime-green euphorbia in the foreground.
Right In this beautiful Irish country garden, a few strong plants grow in bold masses to great effect, among them a white yarrow (*Achillea ptarmica* 'The Pearl'), purple loosestrife (*Lythrum salicaria*), pink phlox, delphiniums and eryngiums.

Top The tiny blue annual sweet pea, *Lathyrus sativus*, is an unusual choice for these wooden plant supports.

Above The wonderful dusky pink oriental poppy 'Patty's Plum' is one of the many intense, slightly sombre shades used to good effect in this garden in Holland, along with indigo monkshood (*Aconitum*) and the deep crimson astrantia, *Astrantia major* 'Hadspen Blood'.

Right Rambling and climbing roses festoon a series of arches in another Dutch garden, underplanted with frothy London pride (*Saxifraga* x *urbium*).

Right In one half of this Wiltshire courtyard garden, geometric beds have been devoted to white and natural-coloured plants. Here, white 'Iceberg' roses mingle with the sweet-scented white rocket *Hesperis matronalis* var. *albiflora*, while the giant feather grass *Stipa gigantea* makes a golden spray on the left – the same warm colour as the sunlit stone walls. The whole composition in shades of white, green and gold is simple yet subtly satisfying – a perfect blend of plants and existing architecture.

larger and more plentiful – and there may also be advantages in terms of design, as plants which associate naturally together are often their best aesthetic partners, too.

So let soil and conditions be your starting point. The style of the garden and its planting will be dictated by what you find. Soil-testing kits which indicate whether your soil is acid or alkaline are available from garden centres, and come with clear instructions, but you will find out just as much, if not more, by looking hard at the soil and its structure, and by studying the surrounding gardens and talking to their owners. Often a garden will have more than one natural habitat, so think about how to incorporate these into the overall design. A sunbaked south-facing terrace near the house would be a perfect spot for Mediterranean-style plantings of silver-leaved

plants and aromatic herbs, for instance; and where the soil is very poor, you could create a gravel garden with plants that will thrive in the shallowest, driest soils. There may be dry shade under large trees, or a more fertile, but nonetheless shady, woodland area just waiting for spring bulbs, bluebells and ferns. A high water table or a stream in the garden will bring its own opportunities and challenges.

Don't feel that this approach to planting is limiting to your garden's potential. Within the constraints of what is naturally feasible, you are absolutely free to create the garden of your dreams – and remember that happy plants make a happy garden.

Colour in the new country garden can be bolder than in traditional schemes. Don't be scared to use combinations that were once

Left *Crambe cordifolia* is a stunning plant for the new country garden, creating clouds of starry white flowers filling an area of 1.8 m (6 ft) high and wide. Here it mingles well with frothy white mock orange (*Philadelphus*).

Right In the same garden, a wonderful mix of white valerian (*Centranthus ruber* 'Albus') and clary sage (*Salvia sclarea* var. *turkestanica*) is crowned by a backlit fountain of *Stipa gigantea*. This trio is particularly well matched in terms of form, colour and texture. *Salvia sclarea* var. *turkestanica* is excellent for new perennial-style gardens. Its pale bracts and pink-flecked flowers on tall stems have an architectural quality, and look good at every stage in their development, from sculptural pendent buds to the dried autumn flower heads. A traditional cottage garden plant, it can also look surprisingly modern. The velvety heart-shaped leaves are also attractive.

deemed clashing: reds next to bright pinks and oranges, for instance, or purples with magenta and lime green. Christopher Lloyd at Great Dixter in East Sussex caused a stir when he replaced his rose garden with scarlet canna lilies (*Canna* x *generalis*) and flame-coloured dahlias some years ago, but these bright, even brash colours are now firmly in fashion. You may even want to devote a special late summer 'Hot Border' to such plants, with red hot pokers, tawny heleniums and rudbeckias, orange and red daylilies, dahlias like the scarlet 'Bishop of Llandaff' with its contrasting dark stems and leaves, and sprays of *Crocosmia* 'Lucifer' like fireworks in the foreground. Intersperse your hot-coloured planting with cooler-coloured

grasses and foliage plants if you need to tone things down.

There has been a huge interest in dark-coloured plants in recent years – in purples so deep they are almost black (as in the gorgeous, much-sought-after iris, 'Black Knight') or the intense velvety reds of *Knautia macedonica*, the daylily *Hemerocallis* 'Little Grapette' or the lovely *Astrantia major* 'Hadspen Blood'. These can create sumptuous effects in the garden not unlike those in Venetian paintings – and contrary to what one might expect, their colours glow richly from the gloomiest shadows. Black and white or silver plants are also popular in new country gardens, and can be used with great wit and style – alternating squares of the strappy

Left The wonderful rambling rose, 'Paul's Himalayan Musk', swamps a potting shed with fragrant soft pink flowers in this Dutch country garden. Though it flowers for just a few weeks of the year, the effect is extraordinarily beautiful, making it a firm favourite among climbing roses. It can also be trained up trees or to form fragrant floral swags between branches or buildings.

More evidence that pastels can create splendid modern effects.

Far left Giant scabious, *Cephalaria gigantea*, is a robust and handsome plant, forming a large open clump in this Dorset plantswoman's garden. Its pale lemon flowers are borne on stems up to 2.4 m (8 ft) high, but its semi-transparent habit, waving and trembling in the slightest breeze, means that it can look equally at home at the front or back of the border. It needs room to spread: each plant forms a clump 1.2 m (4 ft) wide, with dark green deep-cut leaves.

Left In the same garden, pale blue delphinium hybrids look beautiful but ghostly in the low light.

black grass *Ophiopogon planiscapus* 'Nigrescens' with the soft silvery lamb's-ear leaves of *Stachys byzantina*, to form a chessboard effect, for instance, or pots of the near-black tulip 'Queen of Night' interspersed with others of *Tulipa* 'Spring Green', its milky petals shot with fresh green. Some plants have this coveted black and white colouring within the same flower – think of black and white pansies, or the chequerboard *Aquilegia* 'Magpie'.

White-flowering plants will never go out of style – but instead of traditional 'White Gardens', such as the one made famous by Vita Sackville-West at Sissinghurst and much copied ever since, today's country gardeners are creating 'Moon Gardens' filled with pale flowers and foliage that will be seen at their best beneath a summer full moon. Silver and grey foliage plants such as lavenders, *Santolina*, beautiful *Convolvulus cneorum* with its pink-tinged, bell-

like flowers and certain sages, including Russian sage (*Perovskia* 'Blue Spire'), have an integral place in Mediterranean-style and seaside gardens, but are also good foils for some of the deeper pinks and purples. The other great new foliage colour is chartreuse – that seductive greeny-yellow ranging from the sharp lime greens of *Alchemilla mollis* and the golden hop, *Humulus lupulus* 'Aureus', to the duller olive-grey foliage of *Helleborus foetidus* and some euphorbias. It can provide interesting contrasts, both with other greens and hot reds, pinks and oranges.

These hot new colour combinations work so well partly because planting patterns themselves have become bolder. The old-style herbaceous borders relied on small groupings of different plants, perhaps repeated at intervals, while too many sudden contrasts were frowned on. Nowadays, the trend is for bold sweeps and

Above *Sidalcea malviflora* combines an unusual mixture of strong structure with soft delicate colour – a useful modern border plant with flowers that last.

Opposite A pretty mixture of pink foxgloves, lavender and white bleeding heart (*Dicentra spectabilis* 'Alba') thrives in a corner of this former farmyard in Wiltshire, in the shade of a huge copper beech (*Fagus sylvatica* f. *purpurea*). The foxgloves have self-seeded towards the front of the beds, living proof that tall plants need not be confined to the back of the border. The old stone walls, covered in moss and lichen, provide the perfect backdrop for plants.

swathes of colour, so that one type of plant runs into the next, and the combinations are constantly shifting as you walk past. Instead of the strict traditional division between lawn, paths and borders, go for an effect more akin to that of an abstract painting. A wonderful effect can be achieved with just a handful of different plants, used over quite a large area, but giving interesting contrasts in texture, leaf shape and height. The natural clump- or tussock-forming habits of hardy geraniums, for instance, or fountain grasses can be exploited, with drifts of taller, wispier plants infiltrating their ranks. No need to keep tall specimens to the back: spires of foxgloves, delphiniums, monkshood, foxtail lilies or the towering silvery thistle-like Miss Willmott's ghost (*Eryngium giganteum*) work like vertical punctuation marks among the mounds of lower-growing plants. Climbing plants such as roses and clematis can also add height if they are grown up simple obelisks or painted metal supports. The effects work just as well in a formal-style garden, contained within simple geometric beds.

The aim is to build up a shimmering, shifting canvas of plants in which one species is viewed against, or through, another. Spindly plants with a 'see-through' habit are useful here – *Verbena bonariensis*, with its tiny purple flower heads on branching architectural stems; fuzzy *Thalictrum delavayi*; or the giant scabious, *Cephalaria gigantea*, with papery, pale lemon flowers, can even be used in the foreground, where they will create an organza-like effect, sending wild, wayward stems in every direction. Where the old-style border would have a wall at the back and a viewing path along the front, this new looser style can work without a backdrop, and with narrow gravel paths leading right in and through the planting if required. Planting *en masse* has other advantages. If you like lots of flowers in the house, you will always have enough to pick, with no fear of depleting your display. There has been a recent return to the idea of a cutting garden, where all your favourite flowers are grown in a colourful patchwork – not unlike a vegetable plot – with the sole aim of picking to arrange inside. But if you do not have room for a separate cutting area, bold masses of annuals and perennials spread in swathes throughout the garden should ensure a plentiful supply.

One of the most exciting developments in gardening in recent years is the increasing popularity of what has become known as the 'new perennial' style, which makes bold use of ornamental grasses. Building on the principle of using the right plants for the right place, this style of gardening was first espoused by the German gardener and ecologist Karl Foerster at the turn of the last century and is now common in German parks and gardens, and gaining ground in Holland (where Piet Oudolf has his well-known nursery). In the United States, James van Sweden and the German-born Wolfgang Oehme are converting lawn-loving Americans back to prairie-style plants.

With its emphasis on sculptural grasses and wild-looking clumps of perennials, new perennial

planting has a naturalistic beauty which is particularly suited to new country gardens. Grasses grow well in most soils and conditions, and their strappy frond-like leaves and feathery flower heads introduce an exciting range of textures, which are particularly valuable in late summer when many other plants are fading. Of all garden plants, these are the most responsive to changes in light, so place them where the low afternoon sun can shine right through them. A shaft of sunlight illuminating a large clump of *Stipa gigantea* has an effect akin to fireworks, while the pale plumes of pennisetums form a fuzzy golden halo. As the sun moves around and through the different grasses, it will highlight their different shapes and textures. Some, like *Calamagrostis* x *acutiflora* 'Stricta' have a firm upright habit; others, such as the deschampsias, create graceful arcs above the surrounding foliage, like living fountains. The summer-flowering feather grass, *Stipa tenuissima*, has fluffy fronds like tousled fine hair, while *Pennisetum orientale* has fuzzy, furry foxtail seed-heads, and the clump-forming carexes have twirling, twisting tendrils. Their beauty is only intensified by a white outline of winter frost.

Grasses also bring a ravishing sense of movement to the garden, as their swaying foliage and feather-light plumes respond to the slightest breeze. Though most often combined with herbaceous perennials and other wild-looking plants, they are increasingly used to great effect within the clipped hedges and geometric beds of formal gardens, where they soften the boundaries and animate an otherwise static scene.

Grasses remind us of the rhythms of plants in the wild landscape beyond the garden borders – of the wind rippling through fields of oats or

Above Dark maroon flowers of *Geranium phaeum* in the foreground; arching sprays of *Buddleia alternifolia* make a fountain effect in the distance.
Opposite A stunning mixture of alliums and grasses in this modern Wiltshire garden. The pale arching fronds of pheasant's tail grass (*Stipa arundinacea*) in the foreground contrast with the strappy bronze leaves of the New Zealand flax (*Phormium tenax* 'Purpureum') and the silvery wisps of *Stipa tenuissima* to the right. *Stipa gigantea* towers above them all, its oat-like seed-heads lit by the sun and waving in the breeze. This combination of grasses sits well against a backdrop of fields.

rye, or rustling the tufts of thrift on sand dunes. The swishing of their leaves can also bring the ocean to mind.

Grasses grow easily in almost all soil types and require next to no maintenance. But combining them with other plants to create a year-round effect can be hard to get right. They are often grown in a separate area of the garden

geared to peak in late summer and autumn. To extend the interest for as many months of the year as possible, think of grasses emerging from layers of contrasting flowers and foliage. Tall, swaying *Miscanthus sinensis* could shoot up from swathes of the daisy-like flowers of rudbeckia, for instance, providing foliage contrast in spring and a splash of bright yellow flowers

A consummate piece of planting in this Dorset garden. The wild natural effect belies the skill in orchestrating these concentric circles. In the centre is a chamomile lawn, and around that a ring of self-seeded cloud grass mixed with low-growing purple-flowering thymes. A further circle of grasses and low-growing silver-leaved plants is punctuated by spheres of *Allium cristophii*, adding a vertical element to the composition, while spires of foxgloves rise up from mounds of cranesbill geraniums and oregano in the foreground. Gravel paths run between the beds like those in a low foot maze.

in summer, while in autumn, the dried dark cones of the rudbeckia flowers will be silhouetted against the pale, silky ribbons of the grass seed-heads, just waiting for an outline of frost. Or how about the graceful arching stems of *Stipa calamagrostis* swaying above white-starred domes of *Anaphalis triplinervis* (pearly everlasting) and clouds of vivid mauve asters?

Plants that extend the season with dried leaves, attractive flower heads and seeds are crucial to this style of gardening. Piet Oudolf once said, only half jokingly, that a plant is not worth growing unless it looks good when it is dead – and the beauty of dying flowers, frosted leaves and gaunt stems is part of the new perennial aesthetic. *Echinacea*, *Anaphalis*, *Sedum* and

Above Arches tumbling with climbing and rambling roses lead the way to the lawn in this romantic Dutch garden.

Origanum produce long-lasting flower heads which look good all winter long – as well as being appreciated by the birds – and most of the grasses will hold their heads right through the winter. So resist the temptation to wield the shears until February, and then it will be only a few weeks before the new spring foliage starts to appear. For a totally year-round garden, you can fill that gap by underplanting with a carpet of spring bulbs, and perhaps some drumstick alliums for early summer, when the grasses are about knee high. But once they take off you can just stand back and enjoy the show.

The looser, more relaxed style of planting outlined in this chapter has the advantage of being low maintenance. As you are fighting neither the natural conditions in your garden nor the natural growth habits and requirements of the plants, your new country garden should be much easier to maintain than the traditional herbaceous border, while its flowering season is much longer than that of the old-style cottage garden. Leaving plants to seed is not only a boon to the wildlife in your garden, it may also result in some surprises the following year, as old favourites crop up in unexpected places.

Left Blue agapanthus and white rose bay willowherb (*Epilobium angustifolium*) are among the strong plants fighting for space in this spectacular Irish border. Wine-red buttons of *Knautia macedonica* weave among the purple loosestrife (*Lythrum salicaria*) and white campanulas (*C. lactiflora*).

Below Drifts of pink scabious, purple lupins, and the mauve geranium 'Johnson's Blue' look gloriously wild in this Dorset garden, with pink *Rosa rugosa* forming a backdrop. Pale lemon *Cephalaria gigantea* towers at the back, while among the sea of flowers and foliage ornamental alliums such as *A. cristophii* are emerging. Like everything in this garden, the effect looks wonderfully spontaneous, but is in fact carefully maintained.

new formal gardens

Formal designs bring a timeless sense of beauty and order to the garden. Move the formal garden firmly into the twenty-first century by pairing clipped hedges and geometric beds with wild naturalistic planting and ornamental grasses that spill over the edges and sway in the breeze.

A more formal style of gardening, with a strong geometric structure laid out in paths and beds, often outlined in low evergreen hedging, suits all types of architecture, from medieval cottages to Georgian townhouses and much later styles. A new formal garden is also the perfect complement to the clean lines of contemporary architecture. These gardens need not be the enclosed places that were once cultivated between high hedges or walls. There is something timeless and calming about a garden laid out in clipped box and yew – and it looks good all year round, especially after a frost or fall of snow.

Left Topiary gardens are not always strictly clipped and tidied. Here, woolly new growth on beech and box hedging creates a softer atmosphere.
Right In this courtyard garden, square beds edged in box are 'containers' for exuberant planting which spills over the paths in summer. White and pale colours are confined to one side of the garden, while this side is devoted to hot reds and deep shades – the clipped box is the perfect foil for the clouds of flowers and grasses. A central mulberry tree rises from a square of box.

Ordered formality has played a part in garden design from its earliest origins in the terraced water gardens of Persia and Mogul India. From the tiny enclosed herb or physic gardens of medieval monasteries to the radiating pathways of Versailles, earlier formal gardens were usually an attempt to create an earthly expression of a heavenly or metaphysical order – whether found in the healing powers of plants or the divine right of kings. Classical rules of scale, proportion and symmetry were brought into play with this end in view. The results were almost always designed to be seen from above – either by God or from an upstairs window – and there is no doubt that they were impressive, if at times a little rigid.

Contemporary gardening still has a place for formality. Indeed, a strong formal layout, coupled with the restrained use of a few well-chosen plants, makes the perfect setting for today's pared-down sense of style. But, as is the case with planting styles, some important changes have taken place. In particular, interesting

Top and opposite A strictly symmetrical layout of curved beds around a central water feature might traditionally have been planted with low-growing herbaceous plants in pastel colours. In this exciting Herefordshire garden it gives the structural setting for an exuberant mixture of ornamental grasses and wild-looking perennials – a striking modern contrast that is very much in keeping with the spirit of the new country style. Height is provided by the towering seed-heads of *Stipa gigantea* and by metal obelisks, symmetrically placed to anchor the design. As one wanders around the paths between the beds, the colours and textures of the plants can be appreciated in ever-shifting combinations. The geometric elements of this garden are maintained meticulously, which provides a satisfying contrast with the clouds of billowing plants – grass paths are closely mown, making a clear axis to lead the eye down to the little folly at the far end, while the hedges that contain this densely planted area will be clipped straight once they reach the required height. Small formal gardens such as this look stunning viewed from an upstairs window.

Left Box (*Buxus*) is one of the most commonly used plants for topiary – its evergreen leaves and dense habit make it ideal. For a contemporary look, forget complex fiddly designs and stick to simple graphic shapes such as spheres and cubes. Clipped plants in containers are useful for flanking paths or entrances and creating instant order against a backdrop of wilder, more naturalistic planting. They can be moved around the garden to create different effects throughout the year, and can move house with you.

new materials and a dynamic sense of movement have revolutionized the formal garden and brought it firmly into the twenty-first century. Now it is by no means unheard of to have formal gardens featuring concrete or even glass. Modern materials such as galvanized metal or plastic may be used as containers or as edgings for formal beds, while spaces in between may be filled with slate chippings or pebbles. In a 'modern rustic' take on the parterre, beds can even be edged in woven hazel or willow. Where traditional formal gardens were flat and static, today's versions are often strongly sculptural, at times incorporating contemporary art works into the design; at others repeating simple geometric shapes – clipped box cubes or lollipops of bay or privet, for instance – rhythmically across a given area. There is often a vertical element to the design – smart wooden obelisks with white roses trained up them, say, or a long arched pergola covered with a grapevine.

One of the most interesting and influential developments in the new country garden has been the fusion of a formal layout with

Left Traditional formal gardens could be two-dimensional, but modern versions often have a more dynamic, strong upright element. In this garden, a trio of bay trees, clipped as lollipops, make a splendid contrast with the loose mix of *Salvia sclarea* var. *turkestanica* and *Lychnis coronaria* 'Alba' beneath. **Below** The evergreen hedge makes a dark backdrop against which the silver leaves of cardoons and woolly grey spires of mulleins look wonderful.

the wilder, exuberant style of planting described in the previous chapter. Soft mounds or fuzzy clouds of flowers and foliage spill over hedges or edges and blur the boundaries in a beguiling haze of colour, while swaying, shimmering grasses provide the perfect foil to all those straight lines and trimmed shapes.

Formality in the new country garden is not just to be looked at. There is no place here for sterile arrangements of clipped plants and potted shrubs, looking like the pieces in a permanently interrupted game of chess. In today's more relaxed style of gardening, formal design principles and features are harnessed to create useful spaces and atmospheric effects. In a smaller walled garden or terrace near the house, a formal design can create a real 'outside room' for living and eating outdoors, with floor, walls and even a 'ceiling' in the form of a pergola or vine-clad wires overhead. In larger areas the illusion of a living maze of plants and sculpted elements builds up intrigue and mystery. While the layout of traditional gardens meant that visitors to the garden often knew exactly where a path would lead, new formal gardens are places for exploration. Even from inside the house, an avenue of junipers, clipped to form the pillars of a living colonnade, may coax you out to discover a secret seat at the far end. Or a rose-clad pergola

Above In this Herefordshire formal rose garden, evergreen topiary shapes are being trained within simple home-made wooden obelisks – attractive features in themselves which echo the pointed gables of the summerhouse beyond. Symmetrically placed, they animate the garden, almost like sculpture, all year, providing interest after the roses have faded.

Left Chunky evergreen hedges can be used to create a sense of intimacy and enclosure in a garden; they also shelter tender plants from harsh winds.

Right This stunning formal rose garden in Scotland has a simple layout of four rectangular beds around a central sundial. Low clipped box hedges surround the beds like picture frames. Among a foaming sea of low-growing perennials, metal obelisks painted a contrasting dark blue rise up like the masts of ships, planted with climbing roses and clematis. These low clipped hedges form an enclosing windbreak; any higher and they would shut out the view, which forms a stunning backdrop to the garden.

Above left Simple graphic designs are the trademark of new formal style. In this Dutch garden a composition of clipped box in straight lines, swirls and low mounds creates a marvellous feeling of calm. Frequent pruning is needed to preserve the look.

Above centre and right When choosing plants for modern formal gardens, look for those with a strong graphic structure. The delicate hooked petals of the chequered *Aquilegia* 'Magpie' (centre) are a work of art in themselves, as are the deep purple interlocking sections of a Roman artichoke (right). These sultry dark colours are not only fashionable, but they stand out surprisingly well against a backdrop of evergreen hedges, which can frame the flowers like pictures. Intersperse with ornamental grasses for a wilder, naturalistic combination.

intersecting two areas of the garden may tempt you to turn off to one side, to discover a new feature or admire a hidden view.

Old-style formal gardens were often rather intricate affairs. Larger gardens were criss-crossed with complicated paths and secondary axes; smaller parterres had their compartments filled with a froth of different flowering plants or coloured gravels. The key to the contemporary formal garden is simplicity. Stunningly effective gardens can be created using only two or three types of plant, the interest lying in the contrasting shapes and different shades of green, and in shadows cast at different times of day. Simple allées of hawthorn hedges or pleached limes need lead nowhere in particular to invite exploration; the simple enjoyment of sunlight dappled through green leaves overhead and dewy wet grass underfoot can be all the more intense without added distractions. Standard bay trees growing amid squares or circles of clipped box can look wonderfully sculptural against a background of slate or gravel chippings: in spring, the fresh bright green growth on the box will add a whole new dimension to the garden. And for a modern interpretation of the parterre, plant formal edged beds with a sweep of one type or colour of flower – black or white tulips in late spring, for instance, or long-flowering annuals such as *Cosmos* all summer. Or, for the most dramatic contrast of shape and texture, opt for swathes of shimmering ornamental grasses. This approach can work especially well near to the house, linking the formal garden with the wilder landscape beyond the domestic boundaries.

Think, too, of the parts of the formal garden that are not filled in with plants. York stone, limestone, slate and gravel are good foils for formal designs, but there are many other possibilities. Bricks and tiles can be laid in attractive patterns to complement the planting. Or how about a pebble mosaic, with stones of different colours set in swirls or stripes in cement? Chequerboard designs with alternate squares filled with low-growing plants and 'hard' landscaping materials are always eye-catching – try short grasses, sempervivums (houseleeks), chamomile or thyme interspersed with white pebbles, seashells or silvery driftwood. The alternatives are endless.

Below This formal garden in Herefordshire is as rich and exquisite as a jewel-box. The effect is crowded, but never chaotic, as a framework of clipped box hedges and mounds keeps a picturesque mix of apricot roses, fennel and catmint (*Nepeta*) under control. Columns of fastigiate yew mark the entrances and corners, while pots of regale lilies surround the central pond. Seen from an upstairs window, the garden is spread out like a piece of decorative embroidery, the perfect contrast to the countryside beyond.

When planning a formal garden, it is essential to sit down with a pencil and paper and sketch out an overall design, rather than just plunging in and creating a bed here and a water feature there. Begin from the house, considering the views from the doorways and most important rooms. Think about the main axes of the garden, the principal paths, beds and other components. Taking some of their measurements from the house will help anchor the house more subtly in its surroundings: the width of walls or windows, for instance, could be echoed in features on the ground. There may be elements in the nearby landscape you wish to bring into the garden by means of 'orchestrated views' – a church spire on a hilltop, or a circle of trees on a distant ridge. You can then create vistas to focus the eye, by planting hedges or laying paths in these directions, and pruning trees and foliage to open up the views. Some of the traditional characteristics of the formal garden, such as terraces, hedges, allées and rills, can be used to provide links between different levels or separate areas (for more ideas see Designing the Garden, page 82).

Where the traditional formal garden was always strictly symmetrical, modern interpretations need not be so constrained. The layout can be much more abstract – either on graphic lines, like a Mondrian painting, with an underlying tension present between its irregularly shaped elements, or taking inspiration from the organic flowing spaces of Zen gardens. Formal gardens usually mean straight lines and right angles, but there is space in the new country style for sweeping curves, circles, zigzags and crescent moons. Spiral designs recur in gardens of all periods and cultures and can be particularly powerful. Some of these shapes will make simple 'foot mazes' – patterns on the ground composed of low-growing plants and grasses.

Do not feel you should fill every space with plants. Empty areas play an important part in the new formal garden, and have a strong aesthetic and emotional impact. They create the 'breathing spaces' in a walk around the garden – the horticultural equivalent of a sorbet to clear the palate

Above The new formal garden isn't just about straight lines and right angles – find room for curves, circles and spirals too. In this modern Wiltshire garden, a perfect circle of lawn is outlined in box hedging, creating curved beds for pretty cottage-style planting behind. On the right, the curve is taken up in dry stone walling, with beds built into the top for rock plants. The circle sweeps round to a gravel garden in the foreground full of sun lovers such as the orange poppy *Papaver spicatum*, *Origanum* 'Kent Beauty' and eschscholzias. The strong shapes and colours of foxtail lilies (*Eremurus*) and a bronze phormium stand out against the backdrop of the lawn and bring some structure to the surrounding planting.

Above right Although often thought of as cottage-style plants, lupins have a strong architectural structure and can look surprisingly modern in the right environment. Choose the deeper reds, mauves, and plain white and creams instead of pale pinks and lemons.

Right A symphony of soft mauves and rich pinks sits well against the textured greens and clipped box hedges in this courtyard garden in Wiltshire. Note the pleasing variety of shapes – the column of clipped juniper, the squat chunks of hedging, the spears of crocosmia leaves and the openwork metal column up which a dark red rose is climbing – and the contrasting textures of the foliage. Among these, the spires of purple lupins repeat the shape of the juniper behind – visual echoes such as this create subtle aesthetic undercurrents around the garden, like recurring phrases in music.

Left and above Training plants into standards (ball shapes on top of a long straight stem) can be an attractive way to bring structure to a garden. Plants to train include roses, as in this intimate courtyard garden (left), while bay (*Laurus nobilis*, above) lends itself well to the standard shape, and looks good either in a formal border or a kitchen garden.

between the courses of a meal. There can be few things more beautiful than a square pool in a simple hedged space, with just a single jet of water springing up into the sky. Encountered after a much more colourful and crowded area of the garden, such a space is like a lungful of fresh air.

As formal gardens do not rely on flowers for their beauty, they look good all year round. The layout of paths and structural plants will generate an atmosphere in all lights and seasons – magical in frost or snow, freshly greened in spring or shadowy and mysterious after dark. Evergreens are most commonly used for hedges and topiary, but even more seasonal contrasts can be had by using deciduous plants. Beech and hawthorn, for instance, are striking at all stages of their development. When summer is over, the coppery autumn leaves hang on until well into the winter, when the bare branches create a stark beauty all their own, and the new leaves in spring are like tatters of lime silk. Deciduous hedges can be used to create areas of the garden that are 'transparent' in winter – an outside room containing a sculpture or oversized urn, for instance, which is concealed by foliage at other times. A tree or shrub with bright winter berries or foliage would make a good centrepiece for such a garden within the garden.

Formal gardens are often associated with scented plants – herb wheels or rose gardens in particular. As well as providing a pleasing contrast between the different types of foliage and flowers, edged beds may help contain the fragrance of these plants, and will also keep spreaders like mint and *Nepeta* under control. Formal beds are also good foils for plants such as poppies and old roses whose appeal is strictly seasonal. When such blooms are at their ephemeral best, the

Below A combination of formal box hedges and stylish containers has been laid out in part of this Irish garden rather like furniture in an outdoor room. Terracotta planters are raised on blocks to be visible above the neatly clipped box, and flank the gravel path at regular intervals. The pots are planted with white daisies, but could be replanted to give a seasonal display throughout the year, with crocus or narcissus to flower in spring – just one type of flower for all the pots works best. Indeed, restraining the colour scheme to green and white throughout creates an atmosphere of peace and harmony. The painted metal bench at the end of the path must be a lovely place to sit with a book or a drink.

fragile flowers billow like pale luminous clouds above the dark evergreen hedges, softening their edges and blurring the boundaries. After the flowers have faded, the beds' geometric shapes still remain.

The words 'rustic' and 'formal' may not often crop up in the same sentence, but some of the principles of formal gardening may be useful to you even if your taste is much more relaxed and traditionally country in style. Classical proportion and symmetry have survived the centuries just because they are so satisfying and easy on the eye; they can be even more enchanting in unexpected surroundings. Classical placings and pairings will always have an impact – but try to give them a quirky modern twist. Where a traditional design might have a Gothic seat set in a niche in a high

Opposite Modern architecture in this Californian garden meant the opportunity to be especially bold with its design. In a hot climate, white concrete walls are the perfect backdrop for climbing vines or just the wonderful shadows of the plants. The trunks of a row of almond trees have been painted white, to match the retaining walls (and protect against pests). The hard landscaping in this garden is all straight lines and sharp angles, which makes the wild, wayward shapes of the plants stand out all the more.

Above Clipped box hedges contain a rich variety of plant shapes, colours and textures, including the orange-flowered euphorbia, *E. griffithii*, red *Lychnis chalcedonica* and deep red roses. The pale stone of the surrounding buildings creates a light backdrop for these deep, rich colours.

Right The sombre dark reds, purples, bronzes and near-blacks in this stunning border complement the Gothic arches of the pavilion beyond, as do the minaret heads on the topiary hedges.

clipped yew hedge, why not install a simple bleached wood throne in its own twiggy arbour, flanked by a pair of large potted shrubs? A retro stone urn at the end of a vista could be replaced by a modern version in slate, or a simple cairn of stones. And whether you are planting trees or placing tubs on a terrace, pairs or groups of four make a conventionally formal effect, while threes, fives and sevens may be more dynamic.

Being creative with the mower can create interesting effects: imagine a circular glade in the woods, surrounded by ferns and wild flowers – a magical spot for a picnic. In an orchard, leave squares of longer grass around the trees in spring, and plant snowdrops and *Iris sibirica*. Or try making a 'sacred grove' using a simple circle of woodland trees such as silver birch. In his wonderful sculpture garden, Little Sparta in Scotland, the artist Ian Hamilton Finlay has accessorized his grove with a stone inscription saying 'Bring Back the Birch'.

Humour and trickery were traditionally part of the formal garden – remember the *giochi d'acqua* or water games of Italian Renaissance gardens that would soak the unsuspecting visitor who trod on certain stones? There is plenty of scope for wit and whimsy in the modern formal garden. Rather than jets of water, why not use modern

Right Training roses up a painted metal obelisk gives height to this formal bed, as do the pink and white foxgloves that have self-seeded in front. Foxgloves (*Digitalis*) are useful plants in the new formal garden. Though originally woodland plants, their spires of bell-like flowers bring an air of unpredictable elegance to the garden in late spring and summer.
Opposite below White-spotted foxgloves such as *Digitalis purpurea* 'Pam's Choice' are particularly beautiful – this one grows up to 3 m (10 ft) tall.

Above More foxgloves in the foreground of this modern Wiltshire garden. This view illustrates the garden's masterful design, with a patchwork of square beds and grassy paths in what was once a farmyard. Plants traditionally associated with formal gardens, such as clipped box, junipers and lavender are combined with cottage-garden flowers like nepeta and huge towering grasses. The enormous bronze *Phormium tenax* in the background is a bold move, its spiky silhouette sitting well against the sunbaked stone walls. Lavender is another useful plant in formal gardens. Trimmed after flowering, it can be used to create hedges and boxy effects, while left to its own devices, the flower heads make a lovely purple haze above the glaucous grey-green leaves. There are hundreds of lavenders, from white to deep indigo-purple. Pruning will stop them growing woody in the centre, but never cut back to bare wood.

Left Throughout the history of garden design, plants have been used to create structured vistas and frame selected views. In this modern formal design in Ireland, well-grown specimens of Irish yew (*Taxus baccata* 'Fastigiata') create a classical colonnade, leading the eye to a decorative water feature at the end of the path.

Right Steps lead up to an open studio door in this Californian garden. Wisps of *Stipa tenuissima* waft over the edges on the left – this is a good grass for softening the harsh lines of hard landscaping. On the right is a Japanese acer, while asparagus ferns and irises thrive in the warm climate.

Below In this Dutch parterre garden, roses trained over a metal arch form a surround for a view of a stone fountain, making one pause to drink in its beauty before going on.

technology and have steam vapour set on a timer to turn on unexpectedly? Or create exciting lighting effects after dark, projecting coloured images onto walls or lawns. Play games with scale, placing enormous oversized urns in a tiny area, for instance, or using false perspectives. Tapered paths and narrowing pools can make a short garden seem longer, while the ingenious use of mirrors can extend it indefinitely. Framed by arches or door frames in a wall – even an old window frame salvaged from a skip – mirrors really do create the illusion of a new space beyond. They also give you more garden for your money. Run a rill edged with formal hedging right up flush to a mirror in a wall and you double its length; place two mirrors set at right angles in front of a few small clipped yews and you have a full-scale formal garden for the price of a few plants. Mirrors work best set at an angle away from the viewer. Any illusion will be broken if you see yourself reflected too soon in the proceedings; you need to keep a few tricks up your sleeve.

Above An old corrugated iron shepherd's hut on wheels is a picturesque hideaway in this Dorset garden – and could double up as an extra summer bedroom or outdoor office. Painted a delicate shade of green, it also creates a backdrop for planting. It can even be trundled around the garden when you want to ring the changes.

family gardens

The new country garden is a sociable place, filled with children, pets and streams of weekend visitors. A well-designed space can double effortlessly as an outdoor sitting room and dining room as well as a children's living playground – and don't forget to make room for an organic kitchen garden.

The key to designing a garden for all the family is flexibility. Rather than creating fixed and permanent areas for eating out, playing games or watching the sunset, try to build change and adaptability into the design. All functional areas – barbecues, climbing frames and vegetable plots alike – should be attractive features in their own right, and contribute to the overall look and feel of the garden.

Right A shingled summerhouse makes a great play house or secluded spot for adults to enjoy a drink.

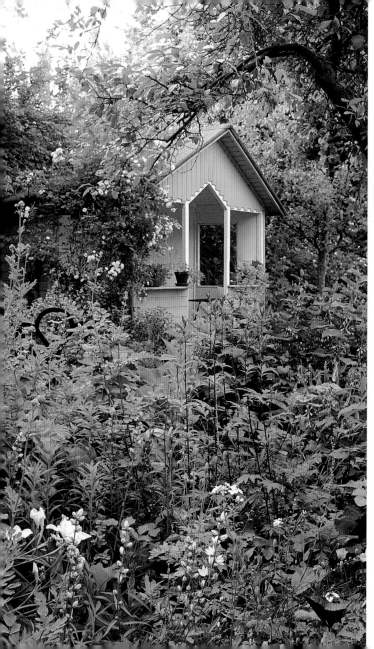

All the family enjoy garden buildings for eating in, playing in, working in or even sleeping in. They needn't be complicated or expensive.

Left and above This Dutch garden's summerhouse is a clever adaptation of a garden shed, with open windows and plants ranged along the ledges. A plain white interior and simple wooden furniture complement the straightforward timber structure and fresh, unaffected colours.

Opposite right Tree houses keep older children happy for hours. A sturdy platform with a ladder up into the trees may be all that is needed, with some sort of retaining fence for safety. Make sure your tree house is structurally sound, and will not harm the tree in which it sits.

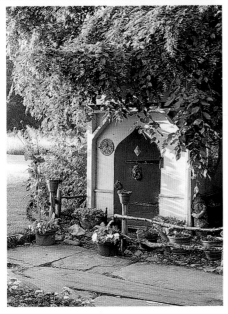

Above This miniature house, with its own fence and front garden, is a decorative part of an eccentric garden. Pretty hideaways can double as follies, or be the focus for a vista.

children If you have the space – and children who love to run and ride around – then, of course, a large area of grass at some distance from the house can be set aside for games. This is the ideal, yet in all but the largest country gardens it is simply unfeasible. Rather than have the main body of the garden strewn with toys, bikes and footballs, not to mention the accompanying skid marks, try to create features that look good in themselves and fulfil a function in the garden, as well as providing a focus for children's games. Fantasy hideouts can double as follies, providing the focal point for a vista or concealing an eyesore – look for inspiration in the local landscape and legends. A castellated tower or rustic tree house is easier on the eye than a plastic slide or Wendy house – and much more fun. They can often be constructed quite cheaply using found wood, leftover bricks or offcuts – materials local to your area will be cheapest and possibly free. Make quite sure the structures are safe, particularly tree houses – and remember you may need to check with local authorities about large-scale permanent structures.

Smaller play features can be conjured up in the same spirit: a simple home-made swing, even a bright wooden or plastic disc on the end of a long knotted chandler's rope, has more sculptural appeal than most shop-bought versions, and sits far more happily in country surroundings. Or what about an organic play feature grown in living willow? Simple bowers and tunnels can be created by sticking coppiced willow wands in the soil (do this between November and March, when they are bare) and weaving between them in a basketwork pattern. You could attend a course or look at specialist books for instructions and ideas. Kids can join in the construction work, and the completed structure looks even more beautiful in spring when the uprights sprout into leaf, creating privacy and mystery within.

Children don't stay young for long, so consider installing or making play features that can change or be converted as they grow. A sandpit sunk in a wooden deck or stone terrace could become a pond in future years, or vice versa. A hideout could end its days as a potting shed, and the site for a swing could become a pretty hanging seat in the shade of a tree. If you have toddlers and younger children, you'll probably want to focus their play around the house, contained by a temporary stake, rope or woven willow fence. When they are older, treat them to a secret adventure playground, screened from the house by swishing bamboo, with ropes, swings and trapezes hanging from branches or sturdy scaffold frames, and a thick mulch of bark chippings on the ground to break any falls.

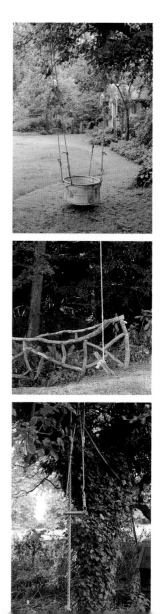

Opposite Swings can be enjoyed by people of all ages – even if the view is not quite as spectacular as this one. Children adore swings but they are also peaceful places for adults to sit and think or read a book. The simplest designs are often the most fun, and sit most happily in a country-style garden. **Above right** Don't just stop at wood. Here, an old tin grape-treading vat has been suspended from a tree to make a safe swing for a baby.

Centre right A section of found timber tied with a knot works almost like a piece of sculpture in this woodland garden, and does not detract from the rustic fence just behind it. **Below right** Plain sturdy constructions of wood and rope look better than plastic, with perhaps a trapeze bar at a different height for the more adventurous.

Above left A stone shelter for animals in this former farmyard has become a splendid summer sitting and dining room. The roof provides shade and shelter, while the open sides afford uninterrupted views of the garden. The elegant metal-frame chairs are comfortable and smart, while a lazy hammock swings nearby.

Above right You can never have too many seats dotted around the garden. Here a matching set of woven wicker chairs makes a lawn into a sociable gathering place.

outdoor eating It makes sense to create an eating area near the house, on a deck or terrace where you can carry things in and out with ease. Sometimes the nicest furniture is the simplest – an old slab of marble or slate on stone supports, or an ancient wooden table, bleached and worn by the weather. For seats, consider simple chunks of wood, which have the graphic, year-round appeal of sculpture, or cheerfully mismatched cricket chairs. If you like to cook outside, why not design your perfect barbecue, with room to warm plates and chop vegetables alongside? For real luxury everyone will love, build a pizza oven into a wall.

One of the joys of living in the country is the pleasure of the seasons and their ever-changing views. At times it is lovely to lay an impromptu lunch or supper elsewhere in the garden – a trestle table or two covered in white cloths and some simple folding chairs are easy to transport to where the apple trees are in blossom, or the all-too-brief roses can be admired. Create an enchanting festive bower, suspending a simple canvas awning from a tree to make extra shade at lunch time, or stretching white fairy lights between the branches at night. Lay flowers on the table and spread blankets on the ground for pets and children. The pilgrimage across the garden – everyone bearing plates and baskets and good things to eat – can form part of the fun.

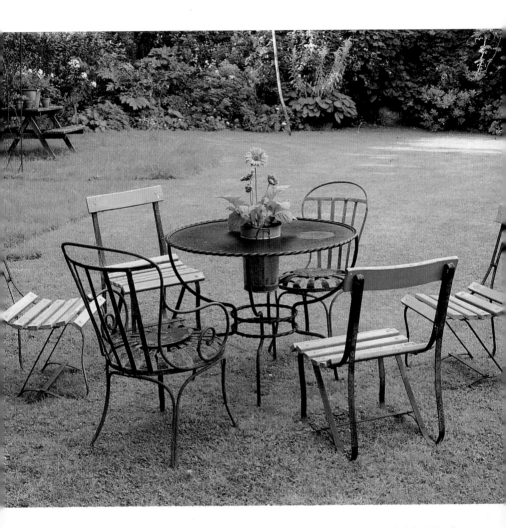

Above Weathered old furniture has the advantage that it can be left outside all year. These old French balloon chairs look wonderfully sculptural against the grass, and would quickly become comfortable with the addition of cushions. A flowerpot sunk into the table can change with the seasons.

A table under a favourite tree makes a perfect place for a family lunch or supper – somehow, home-made food tastes better outdoors. Round tables accommodate large numbers with ease, and an attractive mismatch of old chairs means that more can be added without upsetting the balance. The soft, worn colours of the paint on these folding chairs makes them less intrusive than a brand new set in bright shiny metal or plastic. Meal times apart, this lawn is the domain of the resident goats, who keep it clipped as well as contributing a friendly animal presence to the garden.

Top Functional features should always be decorative in the new country garden. The shelter for chickens in this Dorset garden is a simple amalgamation of old timber, twigs and chicken wire, yet it is as attractive as a rustic summerhouse or piece of sculpture. The hens enjoy it too.

Above Raised beds are an attractive way of growing organic vegetables in limited spaces. You can tend and harvest the crop without treading on, and compacting, the soil. Add a thick layer of garden compost or well-rotted manure every year. Here, the gardener has made the plot look good, with neat canes for runner beans and decorative varieties.

vegetable gardens Eating outside is even better if you are enjoying produce raised in your own garden. The cheapest and best organic fruit and vegetables are those you grow yourself, and for many people this is part of the appeal of living in the country. Rather than hiding your kitchen garden away at the bottom of the garden, make it a feature you are proud of. There are few things as attractive as a French-style potager, with flowers and vegetables growing together in a network of neat paths and beds. But if you opt for more functional raised beds or simple rows, you can make your plot as pretty as possible. Surround it with clipped hedges or woven willow

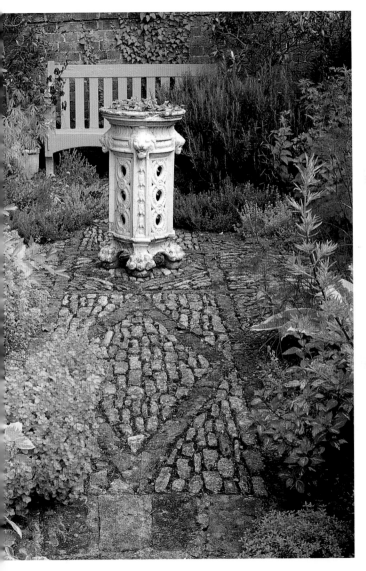

Opposite right Herbs and vegetables grow among the topiary shapes in this attractive Dutch potager. The clipped evergreen hedges and shapes are a decorative reminder that vegetables were traditionally grown within hedged beds to give shelter from harsh winds.

Left A herb garden can be a pleasant place to sit as well as the source of useful culinary ingredients. Herb gardens are traditionally walled or contained spaces, where different herbs are planted in a decorative pattern of beds and paths. On sunny days, the scent of the plants becomes concentrated within the garden – the effect can be quite exhilarating.

Left and above This Dutch vegetable garden is as attractive as it is useful. A clipped arch in the surrounding hedge frames a network of cobbled paths and neat beds, where giants such as globe artichokes tower. Through the gate (left), lime-green curly endive and red oak leaf lettuce, interspersed in geometric beds, add to the display. Terracotta cloches, for forcing chicory and endive, provide height and interest all year round.

Above left The heavily veined leaves of the cabbage family (brassicas) are beautiful, and come in shades from grey-green to purple and almost blue.

Above right A fence of woven coppiced wood creates a beautiful boundary for this vegetable plot, while an additional covering of chicken wire should keep out rabbits. A twiggy arch at the far end supports scented sweet peas for picking. Standard bay trees with plaited trunks stand sentinel at the gate.

fences, and make sculptural beanpoles and plant supports from coppiced hazel twigs. For your own health, and that of the birds and bees that visit your garden, avoid chemical fertilizers and pest controls. Use beer traps for slugs and snails, and investigate biological controls for other unwelcome guests. Growing flowers among the crops can help – for example, pot marigolds and the poached egg plant (*Limnanthes douglasii*) attract hoverflies, whose larvae feed on aphids, while elder and nasturtiums lure blackfly away from other plants. Attracting insects into your plot will also aid pollination, leading to higher yields.

Should you lack the time or inclination to grow vegetables, it is well worth planting a few fruit trees. The blossom will be beautiful in spring, especially if it is underplanted with tiny daffodils, grape hyacinths or fritillaries, and the fruit is undemanding if you choose your varieties well. A good nursery can advise you. Soft fruits such as strawberries and raspberries are also relatively easy, but you'll need a fruit cage, or birds will get the cream of the crop. Pop in some black-, red- and white currants and you have the ingredients for the perfect summer pudding. What better end to a family lunch in the garden?

Country-style gardens have a wild edge to them. Concern for the environment, coupled with the new fashion for naturalistic planting, has led to a revival in wildlife gardening – from sowing your own wildflower meadow to planting a few bushes to encourage butterflies.

wildlife gardens

'Wildlife' gardens and flower meadows have become fashionable in recent years, but as intensive farming methods make fields and hedgerows less hospitable to birds and animals, there is also a real need to make room for wildlife in the garden. Obviously there will be some animals you won't want to welcome, but with a little extra thought and effort, plants, people and a variety of wild creatures can live happily side by side. Deer and wild rabbits are the bane of many country gardeners' lives, and if they went unchecked there would be no gardens at all. So in many areas stout fencing (with at least a foot underground and bent out at right angles to deter tunnelling rabbits) is a crucial starting point. You'll also need to protect seedlings and vulnerable plants from the ravages of slugs and snails. But gardening with nature in mind means being aware of the interconnectedness of all life: there is no use in encouraging birds and toads into your garden if you sprinkle poisonous slug pellets on your potatoes.

Right Clouds of cow parsley (*Anthriscus sylvestris*) billow under the young leaves of a horse chestnut tree in this wonderful Dorset garden. In a garden, cow parsley works well under trees, where it conceals the dying foliage of spring bulbs. Indoors, the flowers look good in huge bunches.

Above left and right Set on a hill above open farmland, the outer reaches of this Wiltshire garden have been designed to blend with views of the agricultural landscape. Further from the house, the mown lawn narrows to a path between long grass and wild flowers, leading to a secret seat where you can sit and admire the prospect.
Opposite and above centre Rampant coarse grasses will usually end up dominating if land is just left to 'go native', though cow parsley and buttercups will usually rise above the competition, and don't be afraid of common daisies (*Bellis perennis*) for your lawn. You may want to encourage the more delicate wild flowers such as ox-eye or moon daisies (*Leucanthemum vulgare*) and corn chamomile (*Anthemis arvensis*, opposite), and papery field poppies (*Papaver rhoeas*, above centre). In order to do this, you may have to remove the normally rich garden topsoil (keep it for other purposes) and sow seed on the poor dusty soil beneath – you can buy mixtures of wildflower seed that have been selected for particular conditions.

Organic growing methods are the best foundations for a successful wildlife garden – well-rotted manure and garden compost will create a healthier soil, teeming with tiny beneficial life forms, than any artificial fertilizers. And natural pest controls, from old-fashioned beer traps sunk in the soil to catch slugs and snails, to nematodes (microscopic organisms) that are watered into the soil or released onto affected plants, are always preferable to chemical sprays that may harm beneficial creatures as well. A well-established wildlife garden should become a miniature ecosystem in itself, with pest control a naturally occurring part of the food chain – thrushes eating snails, for instance, and ladybird larvae feasting on aphids. It may take time to arrive at this ideal state of affairs, though, so be patient. And in the meantime, why not try to encourage a hedgehog or two into your garden? They love eating slugs. Or how about keeping some ducks? One of the founders of Permaculture, a school of organic gardening that aims to create a sustainable, self-perpetuating garden system, using available resources rather than buying in anything from outside, preferred to think of a 'slug problem' as 'a shortage of ducks'.

The best way to encourage a wide range of wildlife into your garden is to create a variety of distinct habitats. Ponds, wetland areas and wildflower meadows will each provide homes for particular creatures, while specific trees and bushes attract different birds and butterflies. If you create only one wildlife feature in your garden, a pond will be the most welcome and will soon be buzzing

Right In the same vein as the garden above, the thistle-like heads of sea hollies (eryngiums) look at home among naturalistic plantings of grasses and wild flowers.

with life. Site it in a sunny area, and make it as large as is feasibly possible – you won't regret it. Unless you have a heavy soil and can 'puddle' the bottom with a layer of natural clay, you will need to use an artificial liner, but turf laid right up to the edges, with a few rocks and stones on the banks, will soon look natural. Make sure the base of the pond is stepped or shallow-sloping on one side, so that creatures such as frogs and toads can hop in and out with ease. They, too, are great devourers of slugs and other pests, and should fill your pond with spawn every spring. Remember to put in oxygenating weeds and aim to cover about a third of the surface in plants with floating leaves, to provide shade and help prevent algae growth. It is extraordinary how quickly a new pond, filled with tap water, attracts wildlife. Adding a jar of water from a neighbour's pond will speed up the process still further. In days you'll see

Left Sometimes the simplest effects are best. Mowing a curved path through long grass claims this area as garden, but retains a feeling of wildness. *Philadelphus* (mock orange) looks good among naturalistic plantings. The long grass obscures the end of the path, creating a welcome air of mystery.

Opposite above A mixture of wild and cultivated plants works well around the borders of this Dorset garden, where the domestic landscape merges with wild fields and woods beyond. Choose your plants carefully – if you select varieties with small delicate flowers that still resemble their wild ancestors, you shouldn't create any unfortunate clashes. Send a rambling rose up into a tree, as here, for a tumbling shower of blooms in summer – after a little initial training up the trunk it should soon take off. These white flowers and their naturalistic growth habit complement the wild daisies in the meadow.

water-boatmen skimming the surface and water snails attached to plants; newts, dragonflies and damselflies will not be slow to follow. Lay a small branch from one side to the other on which birds can perch to drink or preen their feathers in the water.

The borders of your pond can be broadened quite easily to make a marshy or wetland habitat. Extend the lining at a depth of twenty centimetres (eight inches) or so to one side, and fill it with soil. Plant this area with moisture-loving plants such as lady's smock (*Cardamine pratensis*), flag iris and creeping jenny (*Lysimachia nummularia*), to provide shade and feeding areas for various creatures.

Try to free your garden from the tyranny of the lawn. A smooth green lawn may be a great garden tradition – and good for a game of croquet – but ecologically it's a desert. Mown short and doused with chemicals to kill off 'weeds' (which are often native species), lawns have little to offer insects and other wildlife, while constant mowing and sprinkling in summer use up precious fuel and water resources. You may want to keep a lawn as part of your garden, particularly if you have young children or like to

Opposite Strongly shaped flower heads stand out among the delicate flowers and seed-heads of wild flowers and grasses. In a stunning piece of planting, a small orchard of ornamental and fruit trees in this Wiltshire garden has been underplanted with cow parsley and alliums. The starry spheres of *Allium* 'Purple Sensation' are exactly the same pinky mauve as the blossoms on the bare branches of the Judas tree (*Cercis siliquastrum*) behind.

Above left and right Other alliums (left) and monardas (right) would also look good here, and attract pollinating bees to the fruit trees.

play ball games. But try letting one of the borders, or the side that butts onto a wood or wilder area, go 'native' and uncut for one summer. It makes sense to blur the boundaries into the surrounding countryside with an area of wilder planting, and this will be the place where many wild creatures find a home.

Creating a haven for wildlife means more than abandoning the lawnmower, however. If you dream of your own wildflower meadow, ablaze with poppies, corn cockle and luminescent grasses all summer long, this requires a deceptive amount of effort and upkeep. The crucial thing is to encourage the right ratio of grasses, flowers and 'weeds'; the coarser grasses in the average lawn will choke the more attractive delicate plants you want to encourage. Poor soil is

Opposite left The pink moss rose 'William Lobb' is great for naturalistic plantings as it has a wild-looking habit but does lend itself to training.
Left Purple toadflax, *Linaria purpurea*, is an extremely pretty perennial with violet-tinged flowers. It needs good soil in full sun.
Above Astrantias prefer a rich soil and light shade; their delicate, star-like blooms are among the prettiest of garden flowers, and can be found in white and all shades of pink from shell to deepest crimson. They combine very successfully with ornamental grasses.

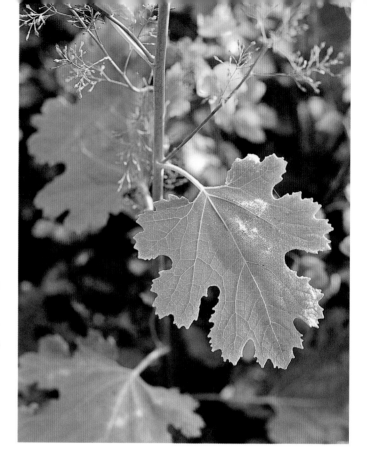

Right The plume poppy (*Macleaya cordata*) is a wonderful perennial that dies down every winter only to put on three metres (ten feet) or more of growth in the course of each summer. Its grey-green leaves have deeply indented outlines like a map of some nameless island, and the bleached buff seed-heads wave like feathers in the wind.

the key to success, and you may need to remove the topsoil before sowing. A sunny well-drained site is the other main requirement. Mixtures of wildflower seed for various conditions and types of meadow can be bought from specialist nurseries, and should come with clear instructions and a precise cutting regime. Persevere for the first year, when the grass may be patchy and the flowers few and far between – and feel free to 'cheat' by popping in some pot-grown ox-eye daisies and cornflowers while the slower-growing plants establish. By the second summer, your efforts should be rewarded by a heavenly haze of flowers and lots of happy bees, birds and butterflies. Mow a narrow curved path through your meadow – the simple contrast between close-cut and wild long grass is endlessly satisfying – and set a secret bench where you can sit and observe the constant comings and goings.

Left and above Many wild plants look beautiful long after their flowers have faded. Poppies have beautiful grey-blue seed-heads with a strong graphic shape which can contribute to a late summer border (left). Leaving the seed-heads is also the easiest way to ensure a repeat show of flowers next year. Papery petals and delicate grasses bring a sense of movement to the garden – they rustle and shimmer in the slightest breeze and catch every fleeting change of light. Position them where early morning or afternoon sun can shine through the fragile inflorescences (above).

Above Even new formal-style gardens can be havens for wildlife – the secret is not to over-clip your hedges or topiary shapes, and to let a variety of flowering plants, which attract beneficial insects, grow into soft mounds. Leaving grass to grow a little longer between mowings will also make a difference – a close-mown lawn is a green desert.

Right This skilful mixture of fuzzy *Calamagrostis brachytricha* with mauve monardas and crimson *Persicaria amplexicaulis* is stunning. The grasses create a shifting screen through which the other plants can be glimpsed.

Just by taking care with the trees and bushes you choose, you can encourage all sorts of new creatures into your garden. Butterflies need particular host plants among which to live and breed, as well as nectar-rich feeding plants like red valerian and buddleia – all attractive in themselves. Any large tree will invite hundreds of birds and insects, but if you are selecting young trees, think about berries for the birds in autumn – a rowan (*Sorbus aucuparia*), crab apple (*Malus*) or hawthorn (*Crataegus monogyna*). Missel thrushes and blackbirds like red or orange berries. Nail nesting boxes in sheltered places, and in winter, hang feeders where cats and squirrels can't intrude. A free-standing bird table in view of the house is a great joy all year.

Above *Pennisetum alopecuroides* has fuzzy seed-heads which catch the light in an incandescent halo on late summer afternoons.

Right A wildflower meadow is not only a wonderful addition to your garden, it is a welcome contribution to the wider landscape, providing a habitat for insects and indigenous creatures, including many whose homes in the wild are under threat from new housing or chemical farming methods. All summer long, the froth of flowers will be quivering with insects and butterflies and humming with life.

PART TWO

elements

designing the garden

garden features

water features

perfect plants

The division of space in a garden into different areas with distinct uses and atmospheres is the essence of garden design. But walls, fences and paths are more than mere boundary markers. They can become attractive garden features in their own right when fashioned creatively from local materials.

designing the garden

All pictures Woven fences in coppiced wood define different areas in this rural garden in Holland. Using natural local materials in a simple yet stylish design is the essence of the new country look. Woven fencing panels keep out the wind while allowing some air to circulate. The moss growing on the fences and picket gate adds to their beauty.

All gardens are designed, to a greater or lesser extent. A well-planned garden shouldn't make you think immediately, 'What a well-designed garden!' It should simply feel like a wonderful place in which to be. However, a badly designed space will seem wrong from the start. Nothing will be where you need it, and its features will be uneasy on the eye. Good garden design may seem elusive, but it is the vital ingredient whereby the various elements of the garden – plants, hard surfaces, practical and aesthetic features – are integrated into a pleasing and well-functioning whole.

before you start Few people have the opportunity, or the budget, to design a garden from scratch. Most of us have to integrate our own ideas within a framework laid out by somebody else, and a degree of compromise may be necessary. If you have a large area to cope with, or have a particularly special feature in mind, it may be a good idea to employ a professional garden designer. Many designers now work on a consultancy basis, where they will charge for an initial visit and a scaled-up drawing of the new design, which can then be given to your own builder or contractor. This can cost less than having the designer oversee the whole process – but, either way, you shouldn't have cause to regret the extra money spent. If you do use a professional garden designer, as a consultant or for the whole project, remember that much of the initial visit will be spent talking – about who uses the garden, how you use it,

Above Promoting a formal look, stone balls flank an opening in this huge copper beech hedge in Ireland. The dark foliage is the perfect foil for the white house beyond, where more stone balls and standard bay trees in pots provide a unifying link in the composition. The woolly growth above will eventually be clipped to follow the arch.

Left A rustic wooden arch surrounded by dense foliage frames a view of a more distant arch – this time just a couple of branches sunk in the soil. Each opening marks a further progression into the wilder landscape beyond the garden.

Opposite Pleached hornbeams form a sort of hedge on stilts, creating a shady allée beside an area of exuberant planting in this Scottish garden. Young trees were planted close together and carefully pruned and trained as they grew, until the upper sections fused to form a solid strip of foliage. The rest of the garden can be glimpsed between the tree trunks, which throw striped shadows across the grassy path. Limes and beeches can also be grown in this way.

Right In this courtyard garden in Wiltshire, the curved section of hedge is yew (*Taxus baccata*), and forms a dense-growing, deep green backdrop for the plants growing on the other side. The lawn is mown in neat stripes to follow the curve of the hedge.

Above Keeping the grass close-mown around the edges of the lawn in this Dutch garden creates a path from which the border can be admired. The area around the swing has been kept short too – the rest is left long for the goats. Woven wood fences are necessary to stop the livestock penetrating the formal gardens. The younger trees also have protective baskets around their trunks.

Left Curved paths and hedges are a graceful way of creating mystery in the garden. As the path sweeps slowly round, the final destination is kept hidden until the last minute. The higher the hedge, the greater the degree of secrecy and privacy attained, of course. The low hedge above has rugosa roses growing in it, a pretty touch well suited to this Dutch family garden.

whether there are particular features, such as water or a summerhouse, that you want to include, and how much maintenance you want to do. Sitting down and talking to others who use the garden is an excellent starting point for planning changes. Try to sit in the garden, or at least in an open doorway, and make notes and sketches of your ideas as you go.

This is not the place to go into detail about the process and principles of designing a garden. There are many specialist books available to guide you on this particular subject, and many of your decisions will be dependent upon the type and size of space you have and how you want to

use it. (See Garden Features on page 96 for ideas on relating the house to the landscape.) You may want to include any or all of the following: a terraced area outside the house, a lawn for lying or playing games on, large areas of naturalistic planting, a formal rose or herb garden, a swimming pool, a vegetable plot, a wildflower meadow or a woodland garden. What is certain is that you will need to divide up the space into different areas – usually by means of fences, walls or hedges – and link them by paths, steps or other features. There are always obvious and more imaginative options when planning and constructing such vital garden elements. Give the matter just a little more thought, and you will be able to come up with the materials and methods that are right for your style of garden.

dividing space All the elements of the new country garden must be in harmony with one another, and suited to its relaxed and creative style. Hedges, walls and fences have their practical purposes, of course – to keep animals and humans in or out, act as a shelter or screen for plants or people, and as a support for climbing or scrambling plants. But they also help to set the house in its surroundings, and create a textured yet regular backdrop for the plants that grow against them. Materials that have some relevance to the house and its nearby landscape are likely to be more successful on all levels. Historically, people have always used local materials for building: wood in forested areas;

Above This beautiful Dutch formal garden is a magical patchwork of paths, allées and secret gardens enclosed by clipped hedges and greenery. The orchestration of the many different shapes and shades of green is quite masterful. Here, tiered balls in clipped box flank an opening in a high yew hedge and lead the eye towards the stone urn in the dappled shadows beyond.

Right In the same garden, trees have been cleverly trained to create a living green pergola above a stone-flagged path. Again, the focus of the axis is a piece of statuary, this time a stone figure.

brick where there is clay; slate, flint and dry stone wherever they are plentiful. If you are lucky enough to have an old wall or well-established hedge in your garden, do keep it – and take care of it by repairing it with similar materials.

But don't be afraid of the new. People have always added new elements to houses and gardens through the centuries, and there is a satisfying honesty about new vernacular materials, properly placed and skilfully crafted. Stone or brick walls give a garden a sense of solidity and permanence and, if they are high enough, of privacy too. Walls of dry stone, red brick, knapped flint or concrete provide different backdrops up which plants can grow – try to match the right colours and textures with the right materials – and a south-facing wall, which retains a lot of heat, makes an ideal habitat for fruit trees or slightly tender plants. Retaining walls can be used to create terraces on sloping ground, sometimes with raised beds in which plants can cascade down a hillside, and steps leading up and down. All walls require concrete foundations, so consult a do-it-yourself manual for details if you want to build your own.

Above The leaves of this zigzag beech hedge will turn a beautiful rustling copper in autumn, and lend a 'see-through' quality to the winter garden. Strong lines such as this work well in conjunction with architecture, and must be trimmed frequently to retain their sharp graphic shapes. The enclosing V shapes of the zigzag create sheltered settings for plants on either side.
Above left Chunky low box hedges define the borders of this paved pool garden in Ireland and help preserve the still, quiet atmosphere created by water. Box's dense habit lends itself to graphic shapes – here cubist hedges and cones contrast beautifully with other foliage in the garden beyond. The containers can be moved around.

Fences are less durable than walls, but they hold endless creative possibilities. If intruders are not a problem, old-fashioned stake fences, or a simple post-and-rail barrier in local wood, are attractive and allow virtually uninterrupted views of the surrounding landscape. More solid fences – woven willows or hurdles, for instance – will act as windbreaks, but can be constructed with strategic gaps or windows to frame views in and out. Willow is ideal for the new country garden. Although it is a traditional technique, woven willow looks fresh and contemporary, and it can be woven in a variety of patterns and styles, from simple basketwork to more complex scalloped edges and spiky finials. You can buy hurdle panels ready made, but why not attend a course to learn how to make them? Or, for a smart modern take on tradition, try painting a picket fence an unusual colour, such as grey or purple. Leave larger than usual gaps between posts so that fragrant plants like lavender and herbs can spill out and release their scent as people brush past. Trellis can work well on top of a solid fence,

Above Local stone was used to make modern dry stone walls in this stylish contemporary garden around a converted Wiltshire barn.

Left A shady corridor linking areas of this Californian garden has been transformed into a feature in its own right, by painting the walls and choosing plants that thrive in these conditions. Climbers are starting to cover the wall, while the palm tree fronds create an archway into the space beyond.

Opposite above Shallow stone steps and a wide gravel path invite exploration of the wilder, naturalistic part of the garden beyond the hedge, while the formal gardens are hidden behind the brick wall on the right. Lavender always looks good spilling onto paths and steps and softens the hard lines and materials.

Opposite below left Scalloping the edges of the grass border to this gravel drive in Herefordshire is a simple but effective way to create a dramatic approach to the house.

Opposite below right Willow fences and hurdle panels are useful ways to divide off areas of the garden while still letting through light and air – and glimpses of the plants within. Modern yet rustic, they fit well into contemporary vegetable gardens. Home-made versions such as this have an unpredictable charm.

Steps are a useful way of connecting different levels in the garden, and can themselves be attractive features.

Above left Stone flags are timeless and romantic, and weather attractively. Wide, shallow treads leave room for self-seeding plants like the pretty daisy *Erigeron karvinskianus* to gather in cracks and spill over edges.

Above right Brick weathers well and quickly. These semi-circular steps, like tiers on a wedding cake, lead from one area of lawn to another. Plants' organic shapes soften the lines of hard landscaping; here, lady's mantle (*Alchemilla mollis*) has self-seeded in the mortar.

to provide extra privacy and support for climbing plants while still allowing air and light through. Forget the flimsy stuff of garden centres and construct chunky custom-built panels from lengths of wood or large bamboo – you can either paint them or let them weather naturally. A trellis panel attached to a deep wooden planter at the base can be moved around the garden like a portable screen.

Hedges make excellent living boundaries and divisions in the new country garden, providing shelter from winds and strong seasonal interest. Mixed-species hedges provide blossom and changing foliage throughout the year, and are a good way to encourage wildlife into the garden, as they offer the variety of nesting sites and food sources that is fast disappearing from the wild. Oak, holly, hawthorn and *Rosa rugosa* might find a place in such a hedge, perhaps with honeysuckle, ivy or clematis twining among them. For a more formal look, grow single-species hedges of box, beech or yew in well-prepared trenches. Plant in staggered double rows for a wider hedge. Bear in mind that you may need to provide a windbreak while the seedlings establish. With certain types of hedging – hawthorn and beech among them – you can allow some of the hedging plants to grow unchecked into trees, or make arches over gates or paths.

Above The impressive reclaimed Georgian stone arch requires a suitably grand approach, and these stone steps, flanked by box hedges and guarded by clipped balls in pots, are elegant yet unpretentious.
Left Timber can also make steps. Here, salvaged railway sleepers contain gravel in which sun-loving echeverias and evening primroses are thriving.

Top and above A well-chosen
collection of chairs animates a garden
and immediately identifies it as a
relaxed and sociable place. Even when
there is no one sitting on them, these
attractive, mismatched old folding
chairs, metal balloon chairs and slatted
cricket seats create a pleasing picture
in the garden, and recall long summer
lunches and candlelit parties.
Right A simple wooden bench invites
the visitor to rest beneath this classical
portico in Ireland. Dark blues and
purples are good choices of paint
colour to sit among foliage.

Left Built-in seats and other features give a garden an air of permanence as well as style. They usually need planning, but sometimes can be fitted into an existing scheme. In this Wiltshire garden, a bench fashioned from salvaged materials has been built into the retaining dry stone wall, overgrown with sun-loving aromatic plants and overlooking a fountain in a modern pool.

Rustic needn't mean retro when it comes to garden features. Modern ideas and unusual materials look just as at home in a country-style garden as in a town one, bringing a contemporary edge to traditional seats, gazebos and plant supports, and blurring the boundaries between arts and crafts.

garden features

No matter how beautiful, a garden that relies purely on plants will lack focus. Seats, summerhouses and sculpture – even plants themselves trimmed into shapes or trained in unusual ways – can be used to lead the eye around the garden, creating areas of intimacy and intrigue and inviting exploration. All garden features, from permanent structures to the smallest seats or plant supports, must be incorporated carefully into the overall design. Good looks alone are not enough: unless the pieces are thoughtfully placed, they will look as if they have landed by parachute. The crucial thing is to avoid the fiddly and fussy. New country style favours strong simple shapes and honest materials.

Above The intense colour of
the beautiful double
Delphinium 'Alice Artindale'
makes it a feature in itself.
Delphiniums come in all
shades of blue and purple,
from white and pale mauves
through glorious two-tone
effects to deepest indigo.

Left One of a pair of curved
seats placed so one can
enjoy an enclosed area of
this Dorset garden, which is
devoted to dramatic
'Venetian' colours – deep
purples and blues and rich
reds and crimsons that glow
with all the sombre
splendour of the velvet
draperies in some grand
Venetian portrait. The bench
resembles antique stone but
is in fact cast concrete
bought from a local garden
centre and weathered.

framing the view Sometimes a garden needs a feature to terminate a vista – to provide the visual focus at the end of an allée of pleached limes, for instance, or to inhabit a woodland glade. If you are thinking of a seat or summerhouse for this purpose, ensure the view in the other direction is similarly attractive, and that the site receives some sun at a useful time of day. If not, a piece of sculpture might sit more happily. At other times it is a matter of fitting a desired feature – a sundial or gazebo, for example – into an existing design.

Be aware of the effect that such features have on visitors: they force them to slow down and linger. A seat will obviously invite a longer stay – and if there is another view to be seen on a different axis, placing the seat at right angles will allow visitors to appreciate it before resuming their route around the garden. Gateways and arbours that frame a view also help to pace the visitor and alert them to the effects of your handiwork. They were used in this way by the grand landscape gardeners of the eighteenth century, but where they would have used a grandiose arch or urn, go for something quieter. Even a pair of simple bare branches, sunk in the ground and crossed overhead to make an impromptu arch will have the effect of saying: 'Stop. Look. See what is here.' Such gateways can also mark the progression from one section of the garden to another, prompting a recognition of the change on both a physical and an emotional level. Different areas can have sharply differing moods, and well-considered sculptures and other features can help prepare for and reflect the changes, or weave a theme – such as death and rebirth, or a particular colour – like a thread throughout the garden.

Left This simply decorated wooden bench is as beautiful as a piece of sculpture. Set in the shade of trees, it affords a view of the summerhouse across the lawn.

Above Hammocks have a wonderful air of laziness and decadence. This cream canvas one is slung on sturdy hooks across the entrance to a former barn – perfectly positioned so the person lying on it can enjoy the scent of the roses climbing up the wall.

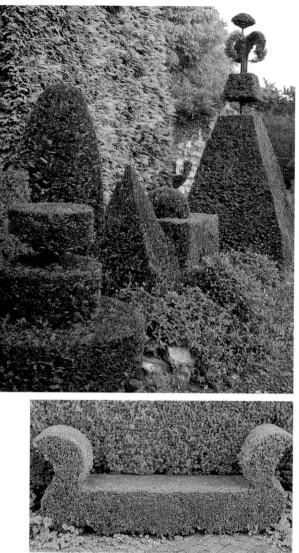

Left Evergreens clipped into drums, cones, cubes and other simple shapes are as closely packed as chess pieces in this Dutch garden. **Below left** A hedge of box has been skilfully trained up around and in front of a stone bench to create this witty seat.

topiary As well as considering static garden features, remember that plants themselves can be transformed into living sculpture. Topiary is often thought of as part of the old-style formal garden, but it has been undergoing a renaissance in recent years as a new generation of gardeners discovers its strong graphic potential. The key to contemporary topiary is to keep the shapes simple: cubes, cones or close-clipped mounds look best, while the impact of a row of holly, bay or box trees clipped as 'lollipop' standards is indisputable. As well as the traditional candidates for topiary, consider more unusual possibilities:

Kilmarnock willows (*Salix caprea* 'Kilmarnock') trimmed into silvery grey mushrooms; winter-flowering *Viburnum tinus* as a fragrant cube; or even gooseberries, redcurrants and blackcurrants as container-grown standards. Topiary has always had a humorous edge, but modern gardeners forgo the giant green teapots and chickens of yesterday in favour of a less obvious approach. Modern topiary relies on strong graphic shapes and subtle visual jokes for impact: leave fiddly figures and comic animals to traditionalists. Close-textured plants such as box can be clipped into living garden furniture, for instance, while

Above Box has been clipped to create a chunky sweeping curve that embraces the enclosed space like a protective arm.
Left Topiary can lend an air of mystery to a garden, particularly if the shapes have been allowed to become slightly overgrown. The truncated column adds to the romantic atmosphere.

Arches and bowers can frame a view, create welcome shade, and support climbing plants. They can also mark the progression from one area to another, making the visitor slow down and notice a change in theme or atmosphere.
Above The nearest bower is totally obscured by leafy hops and *Fallopia*, while the roses scrambling up the far one leave some of the structure visible – both are attractive.
Opposite A series of metal arches frames the view of the tree and countryside beyond. Honeysuckles, clematis and the chocolate-flowered vine, *Akebia quinata*, are trained up them, but they look dramatic left bare.

rows of 'mop-head' standards can grow out of a series of green cubes that read as 'pots'. Sometimes the sheer number and proximity of topiarized plants provides the humour – a jumble of shapes and sizes crowded into an outdoor 'room' like guests at a cocktail party. There is no doubt that plants trained and trimmed in this way take on a mysterious life of their own.

art in the garden An important development in contemporary gardens is the lessening of the old divisions between art and the traditional crafts. A woven willow fence may march round the periphery of a garden like a Giacometti sculpture; rough-hewn blocks of wood may have the appeal of an Anthony Caro but work just as well as seats; a line of bright plant supports, devoid of foliage in winter, can have the impact of a gallery installation. This sort of sculpture is a world away from the stone figures and cast concrete on sale in many garden centres.

Far left What could be more effective, and more suitable, to mark the entrance to this Dorset wildflower meadow than this simplest of wooden arches? A pair of bent branches has been stuck into the soil, almost as if a passing walker had abandoned them, to leave a rustic and fragmented echo of a Gothic arch. Without this unobtrusive entrance, the overgrown path through the meadow might be overlooked.

Left Simple arcs of supple coppiced wood make a splendidly irregular support for sweet peas in this contemporary cutting garden.

Below Roses and hops are excellent choices for growing over arches. In this Dutch garden, a series of metal frames creates a floral tunnel leading from one area to another. The arches will trap the scent of the roses in the summer, making walking beneath them a delight.

Look to young contemporary artists for minimalist, pared-down shapes in stone, wood or metal, or consider local stone carvers or blacksmiths who work with materials gleaned from the surrounding landscape. Or you could commission someone to create a work of art for a specific site. This can become an exciting collaboration, and if you choose an up-and-coming artist you could end up with an affordable one-off piece that might become a collector's item. If you are short on space, think of ways in which a sculpture could double up as a seat, a shelter, or even a bird bath. If you have access to a stone carver, a simple inscription – a fragment of a poem or just a single word – can imbue the surroundings of your piece with talismanic power.

You could even try your hand at creating your own garden art. Take inspiration from artists who work closely with nature, such as Andy Goldsworthy and Richard Long, but try to make the piece your own. Unless you are experienced, it is probably best to keep things simple: an interesting fragment of wood or stone could make a modern menhir; a length of mirror or strangely shaped piece of metal suspended from a tree can lend an air of mystery. Found objects that have been unearthed in the garden and given a new lease of life have a special power – site them where the visitor will want to pause in thought. And a very special quality takes over a garden when the features within it are fashioned from materials found on site. The English garden designer Ivan Hicks, whose work is shown on these pages, makes this approach to garden features his speciality, blurring the distinction between craft and sculpture.

Above Features do not need to be complex to be effective. A simple gilded or mirrored ball, placed in shallow water or where its reflections can be seen, can transform a garden into a setting for magic. Sometimes known as 'witches' balls', these mirrored spheres can reflect the full 360 degrees of the garden, and bounce sunlight into gloomy corners.

Well-placed artworks designed by Ivan Hicks.
Top left A simple cairn of stones on top of an old stone frame has all the power and presence of a piece of modern art, and will weather beautifully in this woodland corner.
Above An old metal hoop from a cartwheel, set among the branches of this ancient apple tree, frames the view beyond.

Left A pile of old flints has been rearranged into a spiral pattern, their white edges contrasting with the carpet of dark moss. Features such as these become an integral part of this Dorset garden, wedded to the site rather than brought in from outside and put down where they look right. For the visitor, walking around the garden, happening upon a series of such features is exciting, like being drawn deeper into a spell.

plant containers Well-chosen containers can also create focal points. Container gardening is gaining ground, particularly in smaller gardens where space is at a premium, or on terraces just outside the house. One of its virtues is that you can move the pots into prime position, or even carry them inside the house, when they are looking at their best. When that show's over, there will be another waiting in the wings, if you aim to plant for a succession of blooms from early spring onwards. If you're clever, the container becomes an integral part of the display – there is real satisfaction in matching the right plants with the right pots. Painted wooden

troughs go well with new country style, while zinc and distressed metal look good with silvery leaved plants like *Santolina*, *Helichrysum* and *Artemisia*. Traditional terracotta contrasts well with glossy evergreens, and now comes in a variety of interesting shapes and textures.

These days there's a wider than ever choice of containers on the market – but some of the most original and eye-catching are those you make yourself. Old or new dustbins, metal buckets, antique fluted laundry bins, and even old watering cans can be pressed into use and arranged in groups for the strongest effects. These one-offs add a quirky character to a

Above These openwork pyramids, made from coppiced hazel wands, are plant supports but have some of the sculptural appeal of a creation by the artist Andy Goldsworthy. Their geometric structure makes an interesting contrast to the wild clouds of campanulas, sedums and geraniums. This Wiltshire garden makes good use of local stone and wood, which helps to build visual and cultural links with the surrounding country.

Simple wooden supports sit well in the garden, and will add height and interest in winter when most plants have died down.

Above An eccentric mix of twigs and fabric strips adorns this sweet pea wigwam, the perfect foil for the wayward mixture of brightly coloured malvas and nasturtiums. Strong verticals like this act as punctuation marks among lower-growing plants.

Left Evergreen bay (*Laurus nobilis*) is being trained into an obelisk shape within this simple wooden structure. It looks good while the plant is growing, and is retained to help with pruning once the desired height and width have been reached.

Right Woven willow teepees are easy to make, or can be bought. Traditionally created as supports for sweet peas in old-fashioned cottage gardens, those with a contemporary twist fit well in the new country garden. The pointed shape is effective against a backdrop of white clouds of *Crambe cordifolia* and delicate white convolvulus.

Above left Terracotta pots age well – pick up old ones from junk shops and house sales. The lichen and moss that forms around the edges is part of their charm.

Left Weathered metal containers are especially appropriate for silver-leaved plants. This collection of old copper and lead planters is filled with helichrysum, alpine dianthus, *Phormium tenax* and the peacock-blue bracts of *Cerinthe major* 'Purpurascens'.

Left Hanging baskets are often sneezed at by fashionable gardeners, but the secret is to choose an attractive, non-plastic basket and fill it with just one thing, not a technicolour mixture of different flowers. Here, a few strawberry plants not only look good, you can enjoy the fruit too.

Above Arrange potted plants on garden furniture as you would bunches of flowers around the house. Part of the fun of container gardening is to match the pot to the plant, choosing colours, shapes and materials that suit the flowers and foliage. In this context it is also important to match the style of containers with the furniture – shiny new pots would look wrong on top of this weathered old table.
Left Bold sculptural plants such as agapanthus suit big containers, and can be moved into prime position when in bloom. When the flowers fade, let something else take their place.

garden. Whatever container you use, drainage is crucial. Too fast and the pots will dry out rapidly in summer and need watering twice a day. Too slow (the most common cause of failure) and the soil will become waterlogged, causing plants' roots to rot. If the pot or container you want to use doesn't have at least one good-sized hole in the bottom, make some with a drill. The holes should then be covered with a flat stone or shards of ceramic to stop liquid running straight out when you water. It's also a good idea to fill the base of the pot with gravel so the roots are never sitting in stagnant water. Add a small piece of charcoal to act as a filter and stop the water smelling.

Gravel on the surface of the soil in pots can look decorative. It also acts as a water-preserving and weed-suppressing mulch. It's worth investigating aquarium gravels in pet shops for unusual colours such as blue and indigo, which look great with the right coloured flowers and foliage. Old scallop or mussel shells can be used for the same purpose in a seaside garden, while mounds of moss would be stunning in damp shade. Local materials that have some sort of resonance with the surrounding landscape should always be first choice when choosing or creating garden features. Things may have changed a great deal since Sir Alexander Pope was writing and gardening in the eighteenth century, but we should still 'consult the genius of the place in all'.

Water features in new country gardens are a far cry from the Peter Pan fountains and miniature waterfalls of the past. Shapes are simple and graphic, and materials are sleek and modern – smooth stone, polished concrete, and even glass. Narrow rills of water can lead the eye around a garden, while small fountains – even just a bamboo spout emptying into a bowl – can transform a quiet corner into a spot for meditation.

water features

Water brings sound, movement and energy to a garden as well as visual beauty. Some country gardeners may be lucky enough to have a natural water feature as part of the garden: a duck pond near the house, perhaps, or a stream running along the boundary. Make the most of them – a stream can be used to create further water features in other parts of the garden. Naturalistic brooks and wildlife ponds work well where the garden runs into the countryside, or in areas of wildflower planting. Nearer the house, take a cue from the architecture, containing the water behind stone-clad walls or trim wooden decking. A stream can become a smart minimalist rill; a mill pond a glassy pool with a single jet of water. Banish images of the kidney-shaped plastic pool liners of the past. Strong graphic shapes such as squares and circles – even triangles and crescent moons – work well, especially in gardens with a 'new formal' feel.

Left This still, shallow geometric pool is the culmination of a journey through a series of different spaces in this garden in the Scottish hills. Edged in stone and surrounded by severe beech hedges, it is a stunning exercise in restraint – its simplicity gives this space at the top of the garden an almost spiritual quality.

Below Still water works as a mirror, reflecting the sky or branches overhead to bring another dimension into the garden. Here in Luxembourg, the mirrored ball works particularly well in water, taking the reflections one step further.

Bottom A spray fountain brings the dynamism of moving water to this garden, shooting water into the sky and creating ever-changing patterns on the pool's surface. Visitors are always drawn to the sound of water in motion.

Above This naturalistic pool, surrounded by rocks and pebbles, is perfect for a gravel garden. Marginal plants like bulrushes, kingcups and flag irises are thriving around the edges, and sit well with the naturalistic planting in the rest of the garden. Comfortable chairs, their wood bleached silver like driftwood, are positioned where the peaceful atmosphere that water in a garden creates can be enjoyed. Rocks and fragments of wood create hiding places for frogs and toads, as well as contributing to the garden's beauty.

Water is often the single most expensive item in a garden redesign, but it is guaranteed to have the most dramatic impact. Plan what you want very carefully. Consider the relationship of water to different areas and their various uses – the sound and sight of running water has an energizing effect on air quality, while still pools and quietly trickling fountains create a more soothing and tranquil atmosphere. Use large concrete stepping stones or simple slate bridges for access. Crossing even a narrow expanse of water can be a dramatic progression from one area of the garden to another: a symbolic entrance to another world. Sculpture placed next to water seems to be imbued with extra power and meaning – or consider a kinetic sculpture, in which moving water is an integral part of the design.

One of the most beautiful aspects of using water in a country garden lies in its reflective potential – trapping the sunshine and reflecting the ever-changing patterns of clouds, flowers and foliage. The simplest shapes are best for this: a square pool, lined with stone flags and bordered by evergreen hedges, or a single circle in a wildflower lawn. Follow the example of the late designer David Hicks and paint the base of a pool midnight blue for more dramatic reflections; plant a border of bright flowers whose reflections will create the effect of an abstract painting shifting on the surface. At night, lighting beneath the water will throw eerily beautiful shadows of fish swimming around the walls.

Right This raised pool in a Californian courtyard is reminiscent of Moorish gardens – in hot climates water is appreciated for its cooling and humidifying effect on the air. The pool is an integral part of the garden, and its tiled edges are wide enough to provide extra seating. The clear blue skies and exuberant, exotic planting are reflected in the pool's dark interior. Dark tiles or paint on the inside walls will increase a pool's reflective capacity, creating the effect of an abstract painting on the surface.

Above left A pond or water feature is a good opportunity to introduce moisture-loving plants to your garden. Some of them are quite spectacular, such as the giant rhubarb, *Gunnera manicata*, with its enormous umbrella-like leaves and spiky prehistoric-looking flower heads in spring. Traditionally grown on the margins of ponds and lakes, it dies down in winter; the dormant crowns will need a mulch of straw as frost protection.

Above right This very successful modern water feature in Wiltshire is bordered by contemporary decking on one side and bricks on the other. Flag irises do well by water, and these white ones are particularly beautiful.

Do not be put off using water for fear of its potential danger to children. Extremely dramatic effects can be achieved using only an inch or two of water. Galvanized metal grilles can be laid over water near the house when very young children are around, with no great detriment to the design – and kids will enjoy the effect of seeming to walk on water. Shallow square pools can be covered over with lockable decking 'lids' or even converted into sandpits for toddlers. Most children will delight in the wildlife visitors such as birds, frogs and toads, and dragonflies and other insects that will be attracted to well-managed water in a garden.

Above Arum lily
(*Zantedeschia aethiopica*).
Left Water features are often
arranged in sequences down
a hillside. In this modern
take on tradition, a still
round pool surrounded by
hedging sits at the top of the
garden, a peaceful place to
look down at the rest. This
secret pool is a reward for
exploring countless green
paths and allées.

Top This candelabra primula, *Primula beesiana*, originally from China, is a stunning plant that does well in moist ground near lakes and ponds. The 60-cm (2-ft) long flower stems hold five to seven whorls of yellow-eyed, red-purple flowers.

Above and left Attractive wild planting around a small pond in this Dutch garden, where orange Welsh poppies (*Meconopsis cambrica*) and lime-green lady's mantle (*Alchemilla mollis*) have self-seeded at the water's edge, and water lilies are about to bloom on the surface. Delphiniums on the opposite bank will echo the pale blue colour of the summerhouse in the distance.

perfect plants

Of course, it is up to you which plants you choose for your garden. Looking at plants wherever you go and noting down those you like best is a good place to start. To give any garden that distinctive 'new country' twist, try selecting a few of your favourites from the groups described on the following pages: everything from Architectural Foliage and Giants in the Border to Accent Plants and the Tiniest Details.

Above Aquilegias are particularly beautiful in their pure white form, as here, or in stylish modern colours such as deep wine red or the fashionable black and white 'Magpie'.

Above Green flowers are always seductive, and those of the Corsican hellebore (*Helleborus argutifolius*) are particularly welcome in the depths of winter. They last well into spring.

Far left *Helenium* 'Moerheim Beauty' has daisy-like flowers in tawny brown and orange. It is a good partner for ornamental grasses in the late summer border.

Left *Echinacea purpurea* Elton Hybrids. Echinaceas' daisy shape is useful in prairie-style planting and makes a wonderful cut flower.

Below Related to cow parsley, but a delightful pink, *Chaerophyllum hirsutum* 'Roseum' is a fashionable addition to the new country garden, its candyfloss blooms reaching 60–90 cm (2–3 ft) in early summer.

hot colours

Sizzling reds and shocking pinks are some of the most fashionable colours for today's gardens. Rather than toning them down with cooler shades and natural tones, turn up the temperature still higher by partnering them with the boldest, brightest oranges. Colours of equally strong intensity don't clash, they create a buzzing halo of energy that the eye can't leave alone. Among the best reds are the bright red yarrow, *Achillea millefolium* 'Fire King'; the scarlet dahlia 'Bishop of Llandaff', with its striking dark foliage; the deep red nasturtiums 'Empress of India' and 'Red Wonder'; the daylily *Hemerocallis* 'Aztec'; and going over into deep crimson, the rose 'Lilli Marlene', the castor oil plant, *Ricinus communis* 'Carmencita', and the rich velvety *Salpiglossis* 'Chocolate Pot'. For pinks, try oriental poppies, magenta mallows and fluffy thalictrums, while stunning oranges include the California poppy, *Eschscholzia californica*; *Lilium* 'Fire King'; and daisy-like gazanias.

Above Even in a photograph, red tulips leap off the page as if in 3D – the effect of bright red against a green ground, which can be used for startling impact in a garden border.

Right The daisy-like flowers of *Arctotis hirsuta* (African daisy) are good for ground cover in a warm spot where you want a sudden shock of colour. Originally from South Africa, they are only half-hardy in this country, and come in rich shades of orange, yellow and pink.
Far right The most fashionable among dahlias, 'Bishop of Llandaff' has brilliant scarlet blooms above beautiful deep burgundy stems and leaves.

Below Achilleas are useful in a mixed border, where their huge saucers of flowers contribute a strong horizontal shape. Very vigorous, they quickly form a large clump, and in strong shades such as the bright red *Achillea* 'Fanal', create a fantastic mass of colour.

Right The California poppy (*Eschscholzia californica*) self-seeds readily in poor, well-drained soil; its papery petals close up on cloudy days. A less common cream variety can also be found – the two look good growing side by side.

Above The rose 'Lilli Marlene' is one of the strongest reds of all the roses. Some other good strong reds are provided by the scarlet species rose, *Rosa moyesii* 'Geranium', the crimson Gallica rose, 'Tuscany Superb', the climbing roses 'Ena Harkness' and 'Cramoisi Supérieur', and the beautiful old Hybrid Perpetual 'Souvenir du Docteur Jamain', whose stunning deep crimson blooms prefer to be out of direct sun.

Above left Commonly known as the Himalayan poppy, *Meconopsis betonicifolia* has startling bright blue flowers. It prefers rich acid woodland conditions.

Above right *Salvia sclarea* var. *turkestanica*, commonly known as clary sage, is an extremely useful plant for the new country border. Though it is a traditional cottage garden plant, its tall spires of pink-flecked petals and bracts have a strong architectural quality and look fantastic when dried in winter. In full bloom, it combines a dramatic size and shape with beautiful filigree detail – a painter could make intricate watercolour studies of the pink stems and pointed pastel flowers. It grows up to 1.5 m (5 ft) tall and makes a bulky candelabrum shape. The plant smells strongly when touched; though some people find its fragrance disagreeable, its essential oil is used in aromatherapy products.

Left The double form of the white peony *Paeonia lactiflora* has stunning pompom heads in late May.

Right The flowers of *Astrantia major* form a neat ruff of petals around a central pincushion. Until recently, astrantias were sadly underrated garden plants, but they are now more widely used, particularly in 'new perennial' planting schemes, where their delicate, starry flowers in subtle shades of white and pink shine out among the foliage of other plants. They are moisture-loving plants, suitable for light woodland, though the darker colours do not show up well in shade.

Below right The white opium poppy (*Papaver somniferum*) looks beautiful shimmering in twilight.

Above *Campanula* 'Burghaltii' is one of the many stunning campanulas in shades from white and speckled pink through to crimson. The palest look good against a dark backdrop, where they light up like lanterns when the light begins to fade.

cool colours

For softer pinks, mauves and blues, look at papery flowers such as oriental poppies, roses and peonies in cooler shades. The names may give clues: peony 'Mother of Pearl', for instance, or the roses 'Great Maiden's Blush' or 'New Dawn'. Irises come in stunning shades from dark *Iris chrysographes* to the pale lilacs of some Siberian or Reticulata varieties. From the many cool-coloured clematis, 'Etoile Violette', 'Elsa Späth' and 'Perle d'Azur' are among the best mauves, and purple-centred white *C. florida* 'Sieboldii' has stylish flowers. Canterbury bells (*Campanula medium*) and monkshood (*Aconitum*) also give strong mauves fading to white. Mix clear blues with darker purples and wine reds, and complement flower colour with silvery grey foliage. Or try subtly two-toned plants such as the pink-tinged forms of *Astrantia major* or the mauve and pink *Salvia sclarea* var. *turkestanica*.

wild new cottage garden

A mix of traditional border plants in bright blowsy colours, strong foliage interest and a few striking vegetables is the key to this look. Poppies and peonies will never be out of place; the dusky oriental poppy 'Patty's Plum' is particularly desirable – its colour is like pink silk dipped in weak tea. Thistle-like plants such as sea holly, *Eryngium alpinum*, with its filigree blue bracts, or magenta-headed *Cirsium rivulare* 'Atropurpureum' are fashionable, and go well with star-like astrantias, in pure white to pink-tinged and the crimson of 'Hadspen Blood' or 'Ruby Wedding'. Vegetables that add height or interesting leaves, like globe artichokes, purple-sprouting broccoli or runner beans on poles or teepees, are welcome among the flowers. Ornamental onions such as *Allium cristophii* and 'Purple Sensation' link vegetables and flowers with style.

Below left The fashionable dusky pink of the oriental poppy, *Papaver orientale* 'Patty's Plum'.

Below right *Phlomis amazonica* is another strong sculptural plant that is becoming more widely known. It looks good among Mediterranean plants and grasses, and because it tolerates dry soils is a good gravel garden choice.

Left Love-in-a-mist or *Nigella* is no less beautiful for being so widespread. Its delicate whiskery blooms are as welcome in the border, where it self-seeds readily, as they are arranged in small posies of flowers about the house.

Below left The deep crimson flowers and attractive leaves of *Rosa moyesii*. This species rose is a superb shrub rose that does well in light shade and is remarkable for the coronet of yellow stamens in the centre of each bloom. It has flagon-shaped, bright red hips in autumn.

Below centre The best cottage gardens are a mix of flowers and vegetables – this leek, left to go to seed, is just bursting into flower.

Below right Chives (*Allium schoenoprasum*) have attractive pink flowers as well as tasty leaves. They make a neat edging plant and look particularly good planted beneath roses.

Above Giant hogweed (*Heracleum mantegazzianum*) is stunning. Growing to more than 3.6 m (12 ft) tall, its architectural form looks impressive at the back of a border or on the fringes of woodland, but it is poisonous, so it is not recommended where children could brush against it.

Right Leeks gone to seed provide height and drama in the border, if not the intense colours of their ornamental allium cousins. Decorative seed-heads are a good way of adding autumn and winter interest.

Left The loose mop-heads of *Hydrangea arborescens* form a blowsy cloud up to 2.4 m (8 ft) tall and wide. Frost-hardy and shade-loving, its snowy white flowers are formed in late spring, emerging from tight clusters of buds and then turning green with age.

Below *Digitalis ferruginea*, sometimes called the rusty foxglove, has small golden brown flowers on sweeping spires that look fantastic in wild or woodland plantings. After the flowers have faded, the dried stems contribute a strong vertical element to the border.

giants in the border

Spires of flowering plants punctuate a bed or border like splendid exclamation marks, even when springing up as singles or small groups near the front of a border. Must-have tall plants include foxgloves, especially the large-flowered white-spotted varieties and the delicate, bronze-flowered *Digitalis ferruginea*; delphiniums in every shade from deep purple to cobalt blue and softest lilac; white and deep purple monkshood (*Aconitum carmichaelii*); peachy foxtail lilies (*Eremurus*) and a host of lupins and salvias. The spherical heads of the larger alliums such as *A. giganteum* and delicate starry *A. cristophii* will vary the form. Tall plants with a semi-transparent habit, like spindly *Verbena bonariensis*, can be used to create a hazy 'screen' or mingle with ornamental grasses.

Above left Thalictrums, with their fuzzy candyfloss blooms, grow to 1.8 m (6 ft) or more and create strong splashes of colour in the border.

Above right The Scotch thistle (*Onopordum acanthium*) has the famous light purple flowers shown on the Scottish national emblem. The plant grows to 3 m (10 ft) or more and has indented prickly leaves.

architectural foliage

Plants with strong foliage give a garden style and identity – and evergreens, of course, are effective right through the winter. Ornamental grasses, among the most fashionable foliage plants for the new country garden, range from the bold silhouettes of giants like *Stipa gigantea* to the silky mauve seed-heads of *Miscanthus sinensis* and the pale fluffy plumes of the pennisetums. Their seed-heads provide stunning effects throughout summer and into autumn and winter, when the low light and an outline of frost show them to great advantage. Other good foliage plants include all the hostas, whose large, ridged leaves have a strong sculptural presence; silvery leaved plants such as senecios, santolinas and helichrysums (all of which do well in strong sun and by the sea), and the wonderful glaucous grey leaves of *Macleaya cordata*, a herbaceous perennial that can top 3.6 m (12 ft) in a summer.

Left The cardoon (*Cynara cardunculus*) has sculptural flower heads on towering stems as well as scrolling silver leaves – all in all a dramatic addition to any border. The blanched stems, but not the heads, are also edible.

Above left The common mullein (*Verbascum*) shoots up a spire of yellow flowers from a rosette of woolly grey-green leaves. Its stately stature and long flowering season make it a desirable addition to the garden – unlike many of the other plants whose flowers form a spire, such as delphiniums, the flowers do not open from the bottom up, but a few at a time along the spike.

Above right One of the many decorative sea hollies, *Eryngium alpinum* has delicate filigree bracts around the central flower head.

Left Hostas are well known as stunning foliage plants – provided you can protect them from slugs, who love to feast on the splendid ridged leaves. There are hundreds of varieties, many offering variegation in the foliage.

Opposite right Moisture-loving *Gunnera manicata*, the giant rhubarb, has an almost prehistoric quality – its leaves open into huge umbrellas many feet across and the flowers resemble miniature Tamil temples.

Left Bearded irises come in an extraordinarily wide range of colours – almost everything except for true red. The dusky purply-red of 'Hell's Fire' is as stunning as it is unusual. Like all bearded irises, it flowers in late spring and associates particularly well with roses; its sword-shaped grey-green foliage is also extremely attractive.

Above *Cerinthe major* 'Purpurascens' is rightly popular for its peacock-blue bracts and electric violet flowers. It is easy to grow and self-seeds readily around the garden.
Right The herbaceous clematis *Clematis integrifolia* has delicate spidery blooms. It can be grown up a support in the border.

unusual accent plants

There will always be plants in a bed or border that cry out to be noticed. Among these are the newly fashionable *Cerinthe major* 'Purpurascens', whose peacock-blue bracts and electric violet flowers are quite irresistible, and partner well with other bright colours. It is easy to grow from seed, and self-seeds readily. Bearded and other irises always cause a stir. Near-black velvety *Iris chrysographes* looks good against the feathery foliage of bronze fennel; the black and lime-green flowers of *Iris tuberosa* and the tawny ochre 'Marshlander' and 'Quechee' are heart-stopping. Turk's-head lilies with their delicately curled petals, bold-flowered clematis and roses like the deep claret 'Tuscany Superb' also draw the eye. Make sure you distribute these 'show-stoppers' throughout the garden, and that something else is waiting in the wings for when their glory fades.

Above left The unusual orange euphorbia, *E. griffithii* 'Fireglow' – once seen, always remembered for its flame-coloured bracts.

Above centre *Lobelia* 'Queen Victoria' has bright scarlet flowers above glamorous bronze foliage. It likes rich deep soil and associates well with dahlias and (as here) crocosmias.

Above right *Potentilla* 'William Rollison' is a truly stunning plant, with splashes of orange at the edges of the bright red petals and attractive foliage. It flowers obligingly all summer.

Above Dahlias are always useful as accent plants – this one is 'Fascination'. 'Conway', 'Pink Pastelle', and 'Wootton Cupid' are other good pink dahlias.

the tiniest details

Getting the details right is one of the crucial aspects of good gardening. Just as the eye needs bold concepts and strong lines to follow when it looks up to take in the whole scene, it also longs, butterfly-like, to settle on one perfect bloom or appreciate the texture of individual leaves and petals. The garden writer Mirabel Osler wittily divided garden visitors into 'crouchers and gapers': 'the former so set on plant spotting that they miss the larger picture, while the latter wander wide-eyed and miss all the details'. Plants that are structurally useful in a border but also offer interesting detail at close range include *Alchemilla mollis*, for its tiny lime-green flowers and habit of collecting dew drops in its fan-shaped leaves, and the many different types of euphorbia, whose fresh green bracts, sometimes with a contrasting deep maroon 'eye', are especially stunning in spring. Look for plants that are interesting at all stages of their unfolding – to watch an allium open over the space of a week or so is a wonder of nature, while roses with attractive hips, or other flowers with sculptural seed-heads, extend the usefulness of the plants long after their blooms have faded. Well positioned, even relatively humble plants such as the elderflower or buttercup can provide stunning effects, bringing some of the wildness of the wider landscape to the garden.

Right Ornamental alliums such as *Allium* 'Purple Sensation' are, in fact, great clusters of tiny flowers that can be seen emerging as minute buds and then opening in the sun. They are attractive at all stages of development, making wonderful dried spheres.
Far right The spotted orchid, *Dactylorhiza elata*, has flower spikes 30 cm (1 ft) high made up of smaller, delicately speckled blooms.
Opposite above left *Allium cristophii* have large balloon-like heads of starry purple flowers. They are one of the most beautiful alliums, whether in full bloom or as a dried seed-head, but their shorter stems make them less easy to use in the border than some of their taller relatives.

Above right The Shirley poppy (*Papaver rhoeas* Shirley Series) comes in unusual pastel shades from white and mother-of-pearl to pinks, reds and bicolours. Their delicate papery blooms are borne on fine hairy stems – horticultural beauty at its most ephemeral.

Left The minaret-like heads of leeks gone to seed are a striking, somehow surreal presence in the garden.

directory

NURSERIES WITH MAIL ORDER

APPLE COURT NURSERY
Hordle Lane
Hordle
Lymington
Hampshire SO41 0HU
(01590 642130)
Wonderful source for ornamental grasses, with a show garden where you can see all the varieties growing. Also stocks hostas, ferns and daylilies.

ARCHITECTURAL PLANTS
Cooks Farm
Nuthurst
Horsham
West Sussex RH13 6LH
(01403 891772)
Bold foliage plants are a speciality; helpful catalogue and knowledgeable staff.

CLAIRE AUSTIN HARDY PLANTS
The Stone House
Coppice Green Lane
Cramp Pool, Shifnal
Shropshire TF11 8PE
(01952 463700)
Great mail-order catalogue where all the plants are illustrated to help beginners choose what they want. Good for peonies.

DAVID AUSTIN ROSES
Bowling Green Lane
Albrighton
Wolverhampton
West Midlands WV7 3HB
(01902 376376)
One of the best rose growers in the country, with an excellent mail-order track record. Catalogue ranges from ancient species to new arrivals.

THE BETH CHATTO GARDENS LTD
Elmstead Market
Colchester
Essex CO7 7DB
(01206 822007)
Plants specially selected for dry and gravel gardens, for shady areas and water gardens – all to be seen thriving in the wonderful display gardens.

COTSWOLD GARDEN FLOWERS
Sands Lane
Badsey
Evesham
Worcestershire WR11 5EZ
(01386 49671)
Specializes in easy and unusual perennials; the excellent catalogue gives plants a 'score' for appearance and easiness.

DOWNDERRY NURSERY
Pillar Box Lane
Hadlow
Tonbridge
Kent TN11 9SW
(01732 810081)
The largest range of lavenders in Britain, set in a walled Victorian garden. Expert advice from the owner and a well-illustrated catalogue.

DE JAGER & SONS
The Nurseries
Staplehurst Road
Marden
Kent TN12 9BP
(01622 831235)
Top quality bulb specialists – well-illustrated catalogue with excellent selection of alliums, irises, tulips and unusual lilies.

OAKOVER NURSERIES
Maidstone Road
Hothfield, Ashford
Kent TN26 1AR
(01233 713016)
Hedging plants, from native hawthorn to box and yew for clipping, hornbeams and trees. All grown on site.

SARAH RAVEN'S CUTTING GARDEN
Perch Hill Farm
Brightling
Robertsbridge
East Sussex TN32 5HP
(0845 0504849)
Bold and brilliant selection of flower seeds, selected for strong shapes and colours for arranging.

THE ROMANTIC GARDEN NURSERY
Swannington
Norwich
Norfolk NR9 5NW
(01603 261488)
All forms of topiary. Not just box and yew – rosemary, lavender and citrus trees in all shapes and sizes.

DERRY WATKINS AT SPECIAL PLANTS
Greenways Lane
Cold Ashton
Chippenham
Wiltshire SN14 8LA
(01225 891686)
Hardy and tender perennials, with lots of conservatory and greenhouse rarities.

THE KITCHEN GARDEN
DEACONS NURSERY
Moor View
Godshill
Isle of Wight PO38 3HW
(01983 840750)
Dessert apples, cider apples, quinces, walnuts, cherries, plums, peaches.

GREEN GARDENER
1 Whitmore Wood
Rendlesham
Suffolk IP12 2US
(01394 420087)
Mail-order suppliers of biological pest controls, including nematodes to prey on slugs, vine weevils and other garden pests.

IDEN CROFT HERBS
Frittenden Road
Staplehurst
Kent TN12 ODH
(01580 891432)
Great collection of herbs. Eleven types of basil, 13 rosemaries, 37 mints – lots of unusual varieties.

THE ORGANIC GARDENING CATALOGUE
Riverdene Business Park
Molesey Road
Hersham
Surrey KT12 4RG
(0845 1301304)
One of the best selections of vegetable seeds, including many organically grown varieties.

SIMPSONS SEEDS
The Walled Garden Nursery
Horningsham
Warminster
Wiltshire BA12 7NQ
(01985 845004)
Famous for their tomatoes – seed for a large number of varieties and many sold as young plants. Also young 'plug' plants of courgettes, aubergines, peppers and cucumbers.

GARDEN ELEMENTS
CAPITAL GARDEN PRODUCTS
(01580 201092)
Topiary wire frames – flat-pack spirals and cones in various sizes.

TOM CLARK
Hurst Barton
Hurst, Martock
Somerset TA12 6JU
(01935 822833)
*Stone carving and
sculpture.*

CLIFTON NURSERIES
5A Clifton Villas
London W9 2PH
(020 7289 6851)
*Good stylish garden
accessories.*

**CROWTHER OF SYON
LODGE**
Busch Corner
London Road
Isleworth TW7 5BH
(020 8560 7978)
*Garden ornaments, from
fountains to planters and
smaller, figurative sculpture.*

**ANTHONY DE GREY
TRELLISES**
Broadhinton Yard
77A North Street
London SW4 0HQ
(020 7738 8866)
*Architectural trellises made
to order, plus arbour seats,
planters and decking.*

**DAVID HARBER
SUNDIALS**
The Sundial Workshop
Valley Farm
Bix, Henley-on-Thames
Oxfordshire RG9 6BW
(01491 576956)
*Sundials in classic and
contemporary designs.*

**HOMESTEAD TIMBER
BUILDINGS**
Wyndham House
Lupton Road
Wallingford
Oxfordshire OX10 9TD
(01491 839379)
*Classic summerhouses,
sheds and garden offices.*

JARDINIQUE
Old Park Farm
Kings Hill
Beech
Alton
Hampshire GU34 4AW
(01420 560055)
*Unusual garden antiques,
handmade pots and more.*

POTS AND PITHOI
The Barns
East Street
Turner's Hill
West Sussex RH10 4QQ
(01342 714793)
*Handmade terracotta urns
made by potters in Crete.
Also a selection of antique
pots and containers.*

ROOM IN THE GARDEN
Oak Cottage
Furzen Lane
Ellens Green
Rudgwick
West Sussex RH12 3AR
(01403 823958)
*Jan Howard's attractive
'rusted' iron plant supports
and obelisks, chunky
wooden furniture and
gorgeous Gothic pavilions,
complete with candelabra.*

TRITON CASTING
Cary Concrete
Torbay Road
Castle Cary
Somerset BA7 7DT
(01963 351653)
*High quality reproduction
stone casting.*

**FLOORS, WALLS AND
FENCES**
BRAMPTON WILLOWS
London Road
Brampton
Beccles
Suffolk NR34 8EB
(01502 575891)
*Woven willow bespoke
fencing, constructed in situ.*

DORSET RECLAMATION
Cow Drove
Bere Regis
Wareham
Dorset BH20 7JZ
(01929 472200)
*Reclaimed flagstones,
pavers and quarry tiles for
making paths and terraces.*

ENGLISH HURDLE
Curload
Stoke St. Gregory
Taunton
Somerset TA3 6JD
(01823 698418)
*Hurdle fence panels, plus
materials for DIY willow
structures and courses.*

FOREST GARDEN
Units 291 & 296 Hartlebury
Trading Estate
Hartlebury
Worcestershire DY10 4JB
(01886 812451)
*Fencing panels and
wooden trellis.*

SOIL AND COMPOST
FAIR FIELD TURF
Fairfield Court
Brookland
Romney Marsh
Kent TN29 9RX
(01797 344731)
*Range of soils and turf
delivered nationwide.*

GLENFIELDS ORGANIC
Glenfield Farm
Haselbury, Crewkerne
Somerset TA18 7NZ
(01460 73251)
Peat-free soil and compost.

GREENFIX LTD
Harcourt Mews
Royal Crescent
Cheltenham
Gloucestershire GL50 3DA
(01242 700092)
*Experts in soil stabilization
and erosion control.*

OUTDOOR LIVING
THE CONRAN SHOP
Michelin House
81 Fulham Road
London SW3 6RD
(020 7589 7401)
*Garden accessories,
including lanterns, metal
buckets and cricket chairs.*

DESIGNERS GUILD
267–71 King's Road
London SW3 5EN
(020 7351 5775)
*Bright fabrics and table
linen, cushions and rugs.*

**GARDEN LIGHTING
COMPANY**
(01706 227525)
*Garden lighting for
entertaining and security.*

GAZE BURVILL
Newtonwood Workshop
Newton Valence
Alton
Hants GU34 3EW
(020 7471 8500)
*Well-made contemporary
and traditional furniture.*

JASON GRIFFITHS
Higher Tideford
Cornworthy
Totnes
Devon TQ9 7HL
(07971 921676)
*Coppiced wood furniture,
plus hurdle panels.*

HABITAT
196 Tottenham Court Road
London W1T 7LG
(020 7631 3880)
*Good for seasonal garden
furniture including simple
folding chairs and tables.*

CATH KIDSTON
8 Clarendon Cross
London W11 4AP
(020 7221 4000)
Retro accessories.

De Brinkhof Garden & Nursery
Dorpsstraat 46
Hernen 6616AJ
Holland
t. +31 487 531 486
Nursery and garden open every Friday and Saturday from 10am to 5pm, from April until the end of September. A small nursery specializing in hardy perennials, old-fashioned and unusual varieties.
Pages: 4, 16r, 20, 28–29al, 42l, 52l, 52–53, 54a, 58–59, 82–83, 86–87, 96al, 100l, 104, 106b-107, 120–121, 121bl

Bryan's Ground Garden Design
t. 01544 260001
www.bryansground.co.uk
Pages: 36r, 39, 44r, 92bl

Lady Tania Compton
Gardening Editor, *House & Garden*
Pages: 2–3, 10bl, 17–19, 23, 30r–31, 41br, 44l, 47ar, 56l, 86b, 100–101

Cooper/Taggart Designs
t. +1 323 256 3048
coopertaggart@earthlink.net
Page: 94r

Huys de Dohm
Heerlen
The Netherlands
t. +31 455 710 470
Pages: 16b, 38l, 48b, 60r, 62l, 63 l, 90l–br, 91r, 102l

Nancy Goslee Power & Associates
1660 Stanford Street
Santa Monica, CA 90404
USA
t. +1 310 264 0266
f. +1 310 264 0268
Pages: 93l, 117r

Isabelle C. Greene, F.A.S.L.A.
Isabelle Greene & Associates
Landscape Architects and Land Planners
2613 De la Vina Street
Santa Barbara, CA 93105
USA
t. +1 805 569 4045
iga@isabellegreene.com
www.gballiance.com/
isabellegreene.html
Page: 45

Ivan Hicks
Garden and Landscape Designer, Land Artist
Hurdley Moor Farm
Middlemarsh
Sherborne
Dorset DTN 5QN
t./f. 01300 345262
ivanhicks@theedge88.
fsnet.co.uk
www.ivanhicks.co.uk
Pages: 108a & bl, 109

Jan Howard
Room in the Garden
Oak Cottage
Furzen Lane
Ellens Green
Rudgwick
West Sussex RH12 3AR
t./f. 01403 823958
janhoward@oakcottage.
demon.co.uk
www.roominthegarden.co.uk
Manufacturers of elegant designs in rusted iron. Garden design services by Jan Howard. Catalogue available.
Pages: 3r, 42r, 57, 96bl, 112al–r, 113

Judy Kameon
Elysian Landscapes
724 Academy Road
Los Angeles, CA 90012
USA
t. +1 323 226 9588
f. +1 323 226 1191
www.elysianlandscapes.com
Page: 49

Peter & Pam Lewis
Garden Design, Restoration & Management
Sticky Wicket
Buckland Newton
Dorchester
Dorset DT2 7BY
t./f. 01300 345476
Pages: Endpapers, 14a, 25, 26–27, 29b, 50–51, 60al, 68a, 78–79, 85l, 106l, 137l

Mill Cottage Plants
Henley Mill
Wookey
Somerset BA5 1AW
t. 01749 676966

Christina Oates
Secret Garden Designs
Fovant Hut
Fovant, nr. Salisbury
Wiltshire SP3 5LN
t. 01722 714756
www.secretgarden
designs.co.uk
Garden designer Christina Oates specializes in imaginative and yet down-to-earth consultancy visits and concept plans.
Pages: 1, 5, 66l, 70, 105, 118r

Sarah Raven's Cutting Garden
Perch Hill Farm
Brightling
Robertsbridge
East Sussex TN32 5HP
t. 01424 838181
f. 01424 838571
info@thecuttinggarden.com
www.thecuttinggarden.com
Pages: 10a, 12–13, 92br, 106ar, 111l

Marc Schoellen
Garden Historian & Amateur Garden Designer
35, route de Colmar-Berg
L-7525 Mersch
Grand-Duché
Luxembourg
t. +352 327 269
Pages: 30l, 67r, 88–89, 102–103, 103r, 108br, 116al, 119l

Tom Stuart-Smith
Landscape Design
Third Floor
43 Clerkenwell Road
London EC1N 5RS
t. 020 7253 2100
Pages: 34–35, 36l, 75, 76l

Derry Watkins
Special Plants
Greenways Lane
Cold Ashton
Chippenham
Wiltshire SN14 8LA
t. 01225 891686
derry@specialplants.net
www.specialplants.net
Opening hours 10.30am to 4.30pm March to September, other times by arrangement; mail order September to March only; please send five second class stamps for catalogue.
Pages: 16a, 24, 40–41l, 60bl, 93r, 97r, 110l, 111r 116bl

picture credits

Key: *a*=above, *b*=below, *l*=left, *r*=right, *c*=centre

All photographs by Melanie Eclare.
Endpapers Sticky Wicket wildlife garden near Dorchester, designed and created by Peter and Pam Lewis; 1 Fovant Hut Garden near Salisbury in Wiltshire was created by garden designer Christina Oates together with her husband Nigel and is open to the public; 2–3 Peter and Sandra Aitken-Quack's garden at Ham Cross Farm near Tisbury, designed by Tania Compton; 3r Jan Howard's garden in Sussex; 4 The garden and nursery De Brinkhof of Riet Brinkhof and Joop Van Den Berk; 5 Fovant Hut Garden near Salisbury in Wiltshire was created by garden designer

Christina Oates together with her husband Nigel and is open to the public; 8–9 Niall Manning and Alastair Morton's garden, Dunard, Fintry, Scotland; 10a Sarah Raven's Cutting Garden in Brightling, designed by Sarah Raven; 10bl Peter and Sandra Aitken-Quack's garden at Ham Cross Farm near Tisbury, designed by Tania Compton; 10br–11 Daphne Shackleton's garden in Co. Cavan, Ireland; 12–13 Sarah Raven's Cutting Garden in Brightling, designed by Sarah Raven; 14a Sticky Wicket wildlife garden near Dorchester, designed and created by Peter and Pam Lewis; 14b Connie Haydon's garden in Dorset; 15 Jim Reynolds' garden 'Butterstream', Co. Meath, Ireland; 16a Derry Watkins' garden in Wiltshire designed by Derry Watkins and her husband, the architect Peter Clegg; 16b Ineke Greve, gardens of 'Huys de Dohm', Heerlen, The Netherlands; 16r The garden and nursery De Brinkhof of Riet Brinkhof and Joop Van Den Berk; 17–19 Peter and Sandra Aitken-Quack's garden at Ham Cross Farm near Tisbury, designed by Tania Compton; 20 The garden and nursery De Brinkhof of

Riet Brinkhof and Joop Van Den Berk; 20r–21 & 21r Connie Haydon's garden in Dorset; 22 Daphne Shackleton's garden in Co. Cavan, Ireland; 23 Peter and Sandra Aitken-Quack's garden at Ham Cross Farm near Tisbury, designed by Tania Compton; 24 Derry Watkins' garden in Wiltshire designed by Derry Watkins and her husband, the architect Peter Clegg; 25 & 26–27 Sticky Wicket wildlife garden near Dorchester, designed and created by Peter and Pam Lewis; 28–29al The garden and nursery De Brinkhof of Riet Brinkhof and Joop Van Den Berk; 29ar Jim Reynolds' garden 'Butterstream', Co. Meath, Ireland; 29b Sticky Wicket wildlife garden near Dorchester, designed and created by Peter and Pam Lewis; 30l Marc Schoellen's garden in Luxembourg called 'La Bergerie'; 30r–31 Peter and Sandra Aitken-Quack's garden at Ham Cross Farm near Tisbury, designed by Tania Compton; 32b & 32a–33 Mr and Mrs James Hepworth's garden in Herefordshire; 33br Jim Reynolds' garden 'Butterstream', Co. Meath, Ireland; 34–35 & 36l Tom Stuart-Smith's garden in Hertfordshire; 36r Bryan's Ground, David Wheeler and Simon Dorrell's garden in Herefordshire; 37 Niall Manning and Alastair Morton's garden, Dunard, Fintry, Scotland; 38l Ineke Greve, gardens of 'Huys de Dohm', Heerlen, The Netherlands; 39 Bryan's Ground, David Wheeler and Simon Dorrell's garden in Herefordshire; 40–41l Derry Watkins' garden in Wiltshire designed by Derry Watkins and her husband, the architect Peter Clegg; 41br Peter and Sandra Aitken-Quack's garden at Ham Cross Farm near Tisbury, designed by Tania Compton; 42l The garden and nursery of De Brinkhof of Riet Brinkhof and Joop Van Den Berk; 42r Jan Howard's garden in Sussex; 43 Jim Reynolds' garden 'Butterstream', Co. Meath, Ireland; 44l Peter and Sandra Aitken-Quack's garden at Ham Cross Farm near Tisbury, designed by Tania Compton; 44r Bryan's Ground, David Wheeler and Simon Dorrell's garden in Herefordshire; 45 Carol Valentine's garden in California, designed by Isabelle Greene, F.A.S.L.A., a California landscape architect; 46–47l Niall Manning and Alastair Morton's garden, Dunard, Fintry, Scotland; 47ar Peter and Sandra Aitken-Quack's garden at Ham Cross Farm near Tisbury, designed by Tania Compton; 48a Jim Reynolds' garden 'Butterstream', Co. Meath, Ireland; 48b Ineke Greve, gardens of 'Huys de Dohm', Heerlen, The Netherlands; 49 Garden in Los Angeles designed by Judy Kameon – Elysian Landscapes; 50–51 Sticky Wicket wildlife garden near Dorchester, designed and created by Peter and Pam Lewis; 51b The Farrell family, Woodnewton; 52l & 52–53 The garden and nursery De Brinkhof of Riet Brinkhof and Joop Van Den Berk; 53ar The Farrell family, Woodnewton; 53b Mr and Mrs James Hepworth's garden in Herefordshire; 54a The garden and nursery De Brinkhof of Riet Brinkhof and Joop Van Den Berk; 54b The Farrell family, Woodnewton; 54c & 55 Mr and Mrs James Hepworth's garden in Herefordshire; 56l Peter and Sandra Aitken-Quack's garden at Ham Cross Farm near Tisbury, designed by Tania Compton; 56r Jim Reynold's garden 'Butterstream', Co. Meath, Ireland; 57 Jan Howard's garden in Sussex; 58–59 The garden and nursery De Brinkhof of Riet Brinkhof and Joop Van Den Berk; 60al Sticky Wicket wildlife garden near Dorchester, designed and created by Peter and Pam Lewis; 60bl Derry Watkins' garden in Wiltshire designed by Derry Watkins and her husband, the architect Peter Clegg; 60r Ineke Greve, gardens of 'Huys de Dohm', Heerlen, The Netherlands; 61 Mr and Mrs James Hepworth's garden in Herefordshire; 62l Ineke Greve, gardens of 'Huys de Dohm' Heerlen, The Netherlands; 63r Connie Haydon's garden in Dorset; 64–65 Cranborne Manor, Dorset; 66l Fovant Hut Garden near Salisbury in Wiltshire was created by garden designer Christina Oates together with her husband Nigel and is open to the public; 67r Marc Schoellen's garden in Luxembourg called 'La Bergerie'; 68a Sticky Wicket wildlife garden near Dorchester, designed and created by Peter and Pam Lewis; 68r–69 Niall Manning and Alastair Morton's garden, Dunard, Fintry, Scotland; 70 Fovant Hut Garden near Salisbury in Wiltshire was created by garden designer Christina Oates together with her husband

Nigel and is open to the public; 75 & 76l Tom Stuart-Smith's garden in Hertfordshire; 76r–77 Connie Haydon's garden in Dorset; 78–79 Sticky Wicket wildlife garden near Dorchester, designed and created by Peter and Pam Lewis; 80–81 Connie Haydon's garden in Dorset; 82–83 The garden and nursery De Brinkhof of Riet Brinkhof and Joop Van Den Berk; 84 Niall Manning and Alastair Morton's garden, Dunard, Fintry, Scotland; 85l Sticky Wicket wildlife garden near Dorchester, designed and created by Peter and Pam Lewis; 85r Jim Reynolds' garden 'Butterstream', Co. Meath, Ireland; 86–87 The garden and nursery De Brinkhof of Riet Brinkhof and Joop Van Den Berk; 86b Peter and Sandra Aitken-Quack's garden at Ham Cross Farm near Tisbury, designed by Tania Compton; 88–89 Marc Schoellen's garden in Luxembourg called 'La Bergerie'; 90l–br & 91r Ineke Greve, gardens of 'Huys de Dohm', Heerlen, The Netherlands; 90ar–91l Jim Reynolds' garden 'Butterstream', Co. Meath, Ireland; 92a Niall Manning and Alastair Morton's garden, Dunard, Fintry, Scotland; 92bl Bryan's Ground, David Wheeler and Simon Dorrell's garden in Herefordshire; 92br Sarah Raven's Cutting Garden in Brightling, designed by Sarah Raven; 93l Nancy Goslee Power, garden designer, Los Angeles; 93r Derry Watkins' garden in Wiltshire designed by Derry Watkins and her husband, the architect Peter Clegg; 94l Mr and Mrs James Hepworth's garden in Herefordshire; 94r Connie Haydon's garden in Dorset; 95l Laura Cooper and Nick Taggart's Los Angeles garden, designed by Cooper/Taggart Designs; 95r Jim Reynolds' garden 'Butterstream', Co. Meath, Ireland; 96al The garden and nursery De Brinkhof of Riet Brinkhof and Joop Van Den Berk; 96bl Jan Howard's garden in Sussex; 96r–97l Jim Reynolds' garden 'Butterstream', Co. Meath, Ireland; 97r Derry Watkins' garden in Wiltshire designed by Derry Watkins and her husband, the architect Peter Clegg; Connie Haydon's garden in Dorset; 100l The garden and nursery De Brinkhof of Riet Brinkhof and Joop Van Den Berk; 100–101 Peter and Sandra Aitken-Quack's garden at Ham Cross Farm near Tisbury, designed by Tania Compton; 102l Ineke Greve, gardens of 'Huys de Dohm', Heerlen, The Netherlands; 102–103 & 103r Marc Schoellen's garden in Luxembourg called 'La Bergerie'; 104 The garden and nursery De Brinkhof of Riet Brinkhof and Joop Van Den Berk; 105 Fovant Hut Garden near Salisbury in Wiltshire was created by garden designer Christina Oates together with her husband Nigel and is open to the public; 106l Sticky Wicket wildlife garden near Dorchester, designed and created by Peter and Pam Lewis; 106ar Sarah Raven's Cutting Garden in Brightling, designed by Sarah Raven; 106b–107 The garden and nursery De Brinkhof of Riet Brinkhof and Joop Van Den Berk; 108a & bl Mart Barlow's garden designed by Ivan Hicks; 108br Marc Schoellen's garden in Luxembourg called 'La Bergerie'; 109 Mart Barlow's garden designed by Ivan Hicks; 110l Derry Watkins' garden in Wiltshire designed by Derry Watkins and her husband, the architect Peter Clegg; 110r Jim Reynolds' garden 'Butterstream', Co. Meath, Ireland; 111l Sarah Raven's Cutting Garden in Brightling, designed by Sarah Raven; 111r Derry Watkins' garden in Wiltshire designed by Derry Watkins and her husband, the architect Peter Clegg; 112al–r & 113 Jan Howard's garden in Sussex; 112bl Mr and Mrs James Hepworth's garden in Herefordshire; 114–115 Niall Manning and Alastair Morton's garden, Dunard, Fintry, Scotland; 116al Marc Schoellen's garden in Luxembourg called 'La Bergerie'; 116bl Derry Watkins' garden in Wiltshire designed by Derry Watkins and her husband, the architect Peter Clegg; 116–117 The Farrell family, Woodnewton; 117r Nancy Goslee Power, garden designer, Los Angeles; 118r Fovant Hut Garden near Salisbury in Wiltshire was created by garden designer Christina Oates together with her husband Nigel and is open to the public; 119l Marc Schoellen's garden in Luxembourg called 'La Bergerie'; 120–121 & 121bl The garden and nursery De Brinkhof of Riet Brinkhof and Joop Van Den Berk; 137l Sticky Wicket wildlife garden near Dorchester, designed and created by Peter and Pam Lewis.

index

Figures in *italics* refer to captions.

acknowledgments

We would both like to thank the many garden owners and designers who so kindly allowed us to feature their homes and work in this book – it goes without saying that without them, this book would never have been possible. Many were also extremely generous with their time during our visits, and Melanie would particularly like to thank the people who allowed her to stay with them while she was photographing the gardens. So enormous thanks to: Peter and Sandra Aitken-Quack, Mart Barlow, Riet Brinkhof and Joop Van Den Berk, Tania Compton, Laura Cooper and Nick Taggart, Peter Farrell and family, Connie Haydon, James and Anne Hepworth and Anthony Brooks, Ivan Hicks, Jan Howard, Nancy Goslee Power, Isabelle Greene, Ineke Greve, Judy Kameon, Pam and Peter Lewis, Niall Manning and Alastair Morton, Christina and Nigel Oates, Sarah Raven and Adam Nicolson, Jim Reynolds, Marc Schoellen, Daphne Shackleton, Tom Stuart-Smith and family, Carol Valentine, Derry Watkins and Peter Clegg, David Wheeler and Simon Dorrell. Melanie would like to say an extra special thank you to Frances Anderton in Los Angeles for helping with gardening contacts and for having her to stay for ten days while she photographed. Elspeth would like to give a big thank you to Marianne Majerus for putting her in touch with Marc Schoellen in Luxembourg. And last but not least, we are extremely grateful to everyone at Ryland Peters and Small who has helped put the book together and especially Alison Starling who first approached us with the idea.

Elspeth Thompson and Melanie Eclare